what do you think of our book?
we would be very grateful if you could let us have a feedback.
Don't forget it

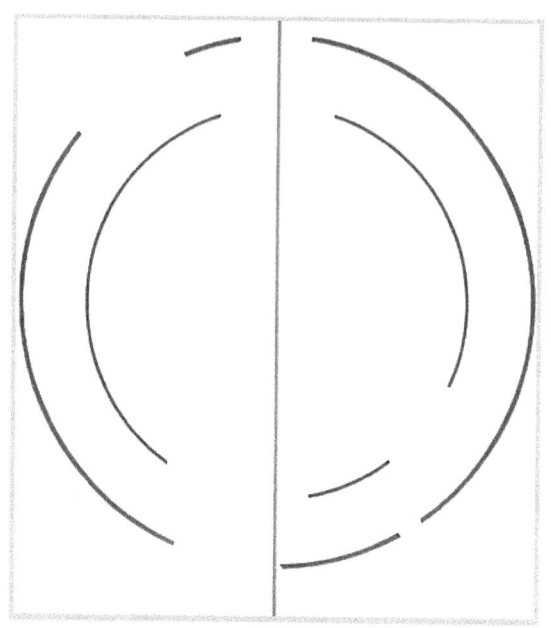

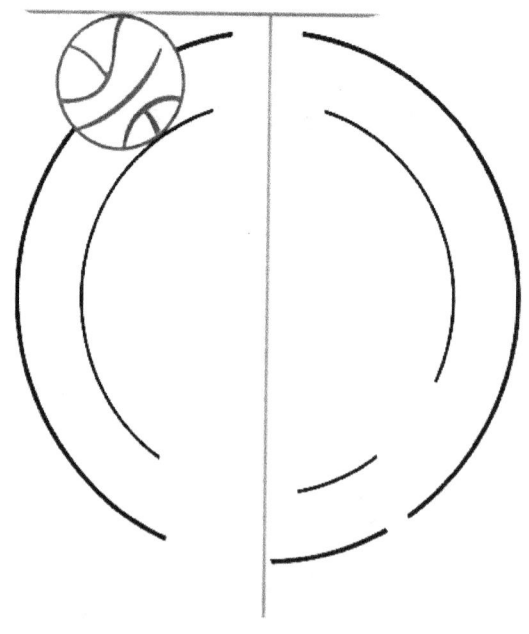

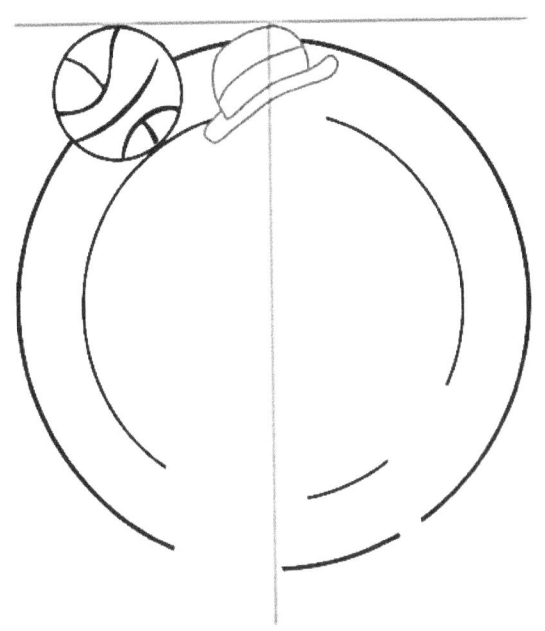

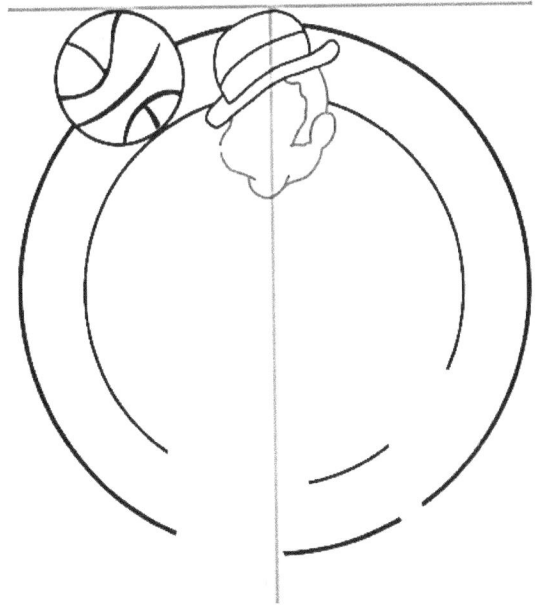

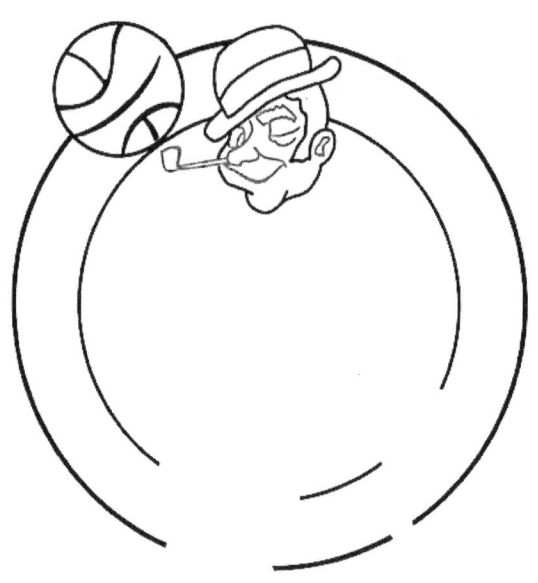
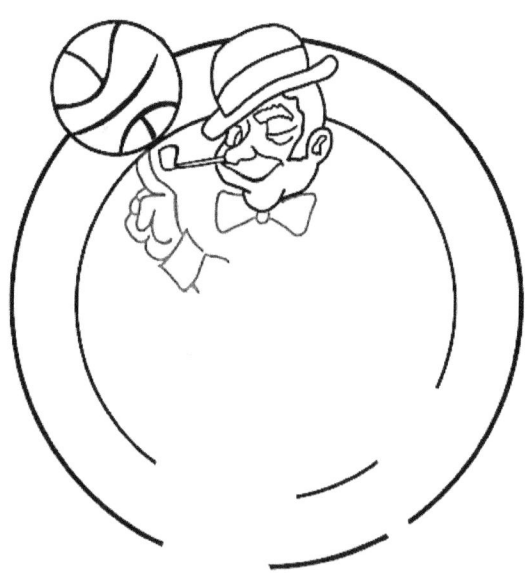

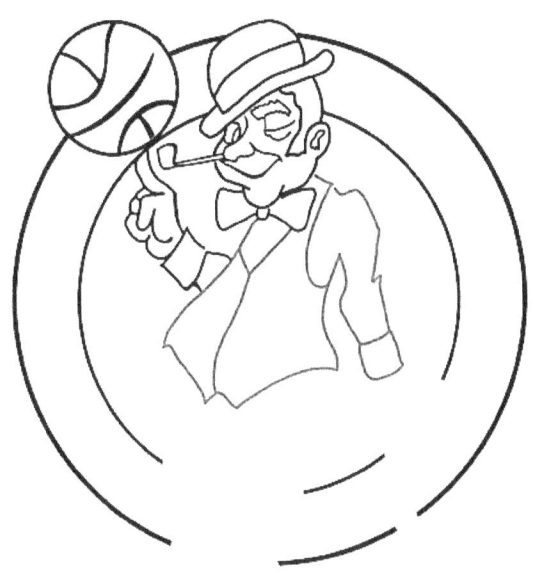
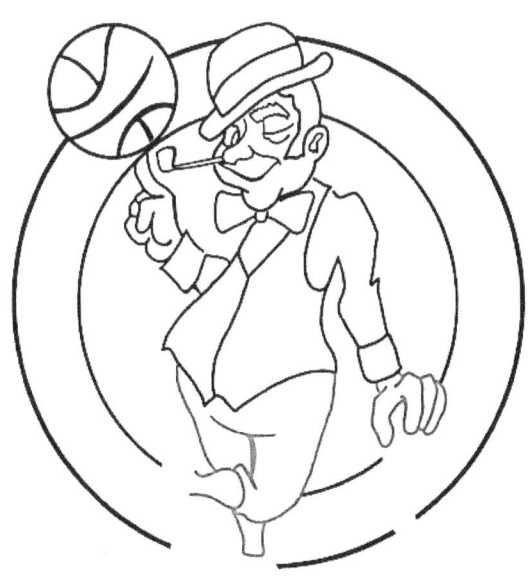

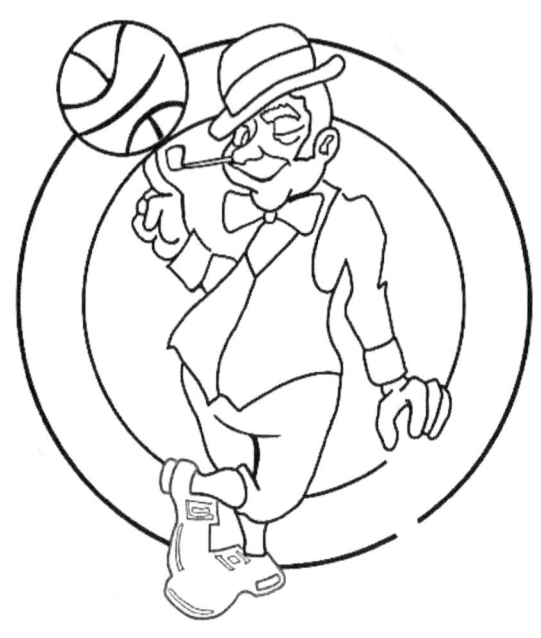

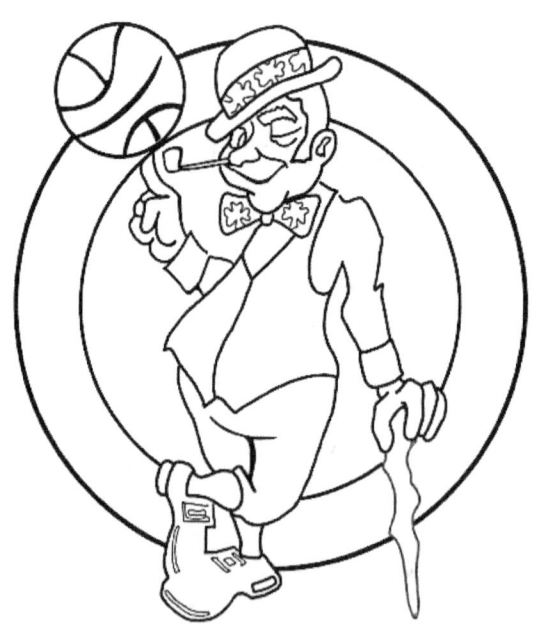

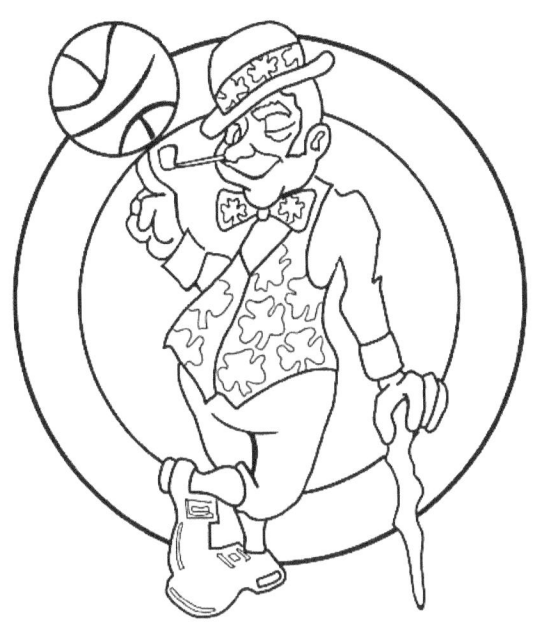
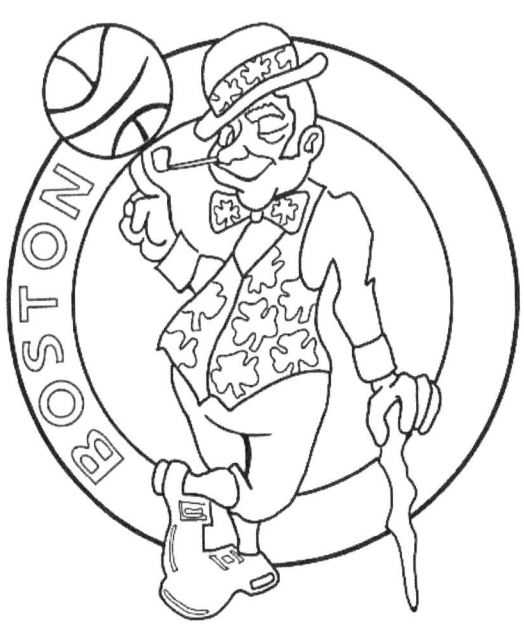

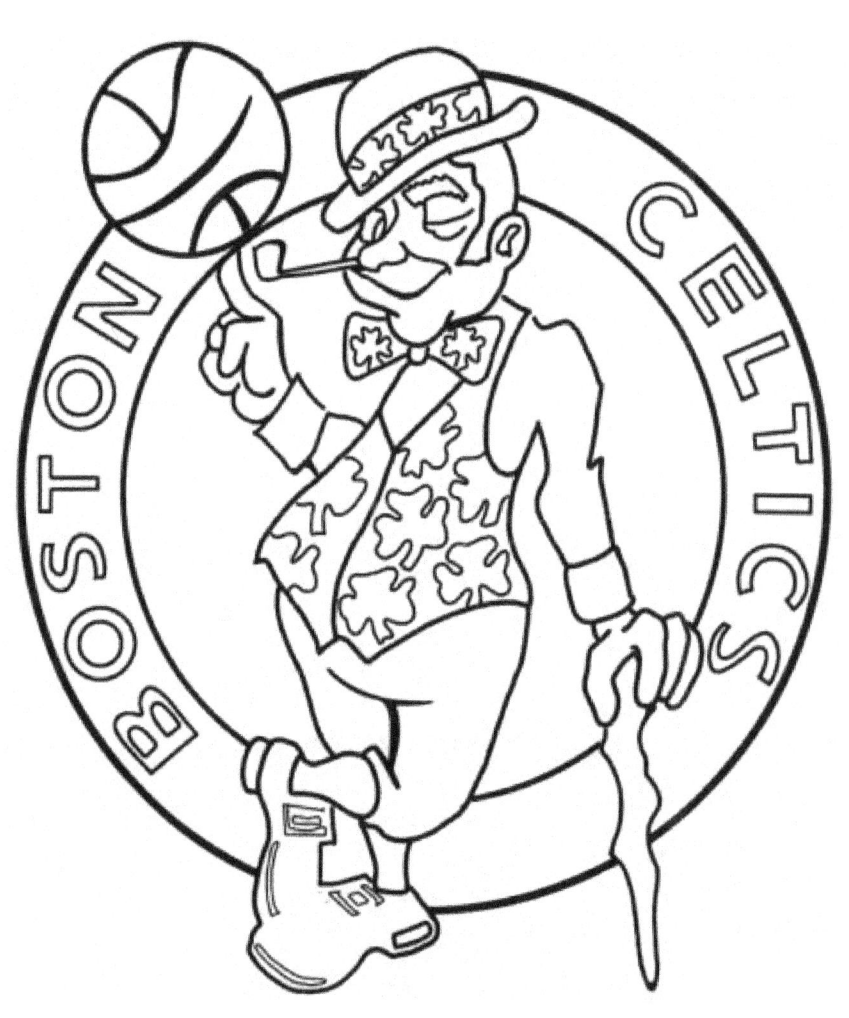

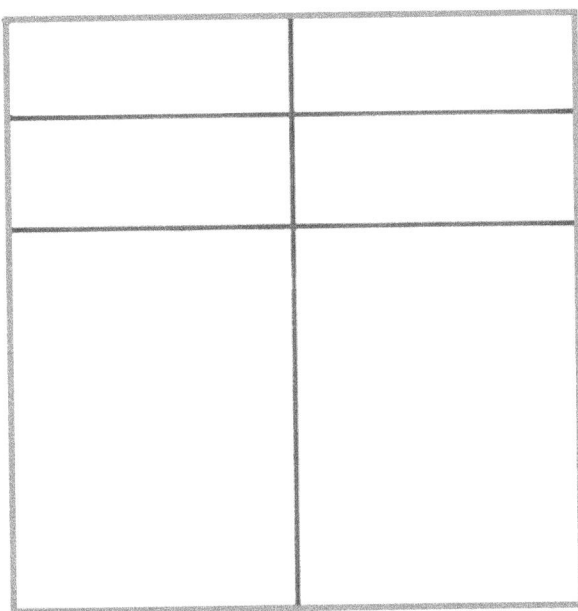

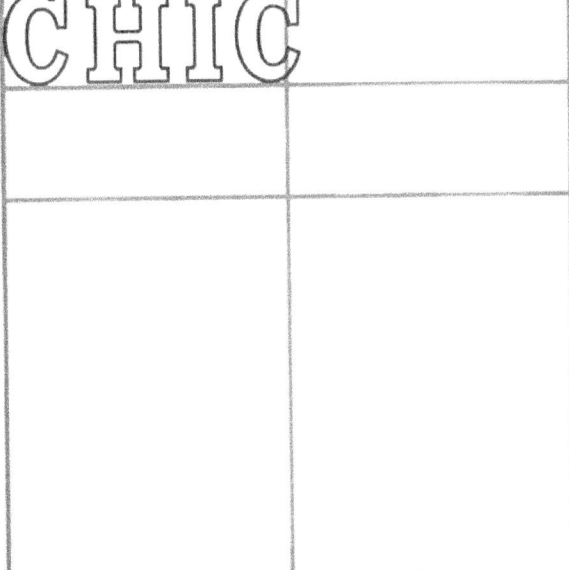

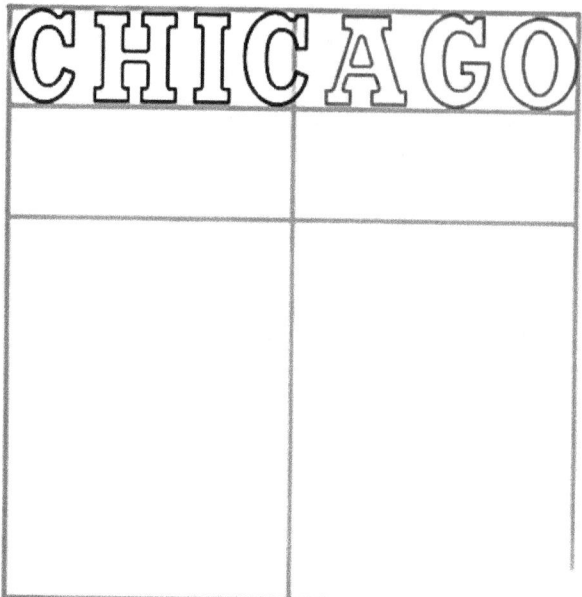

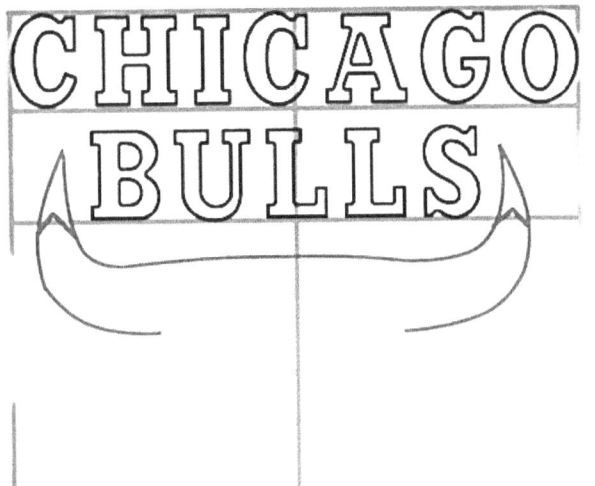

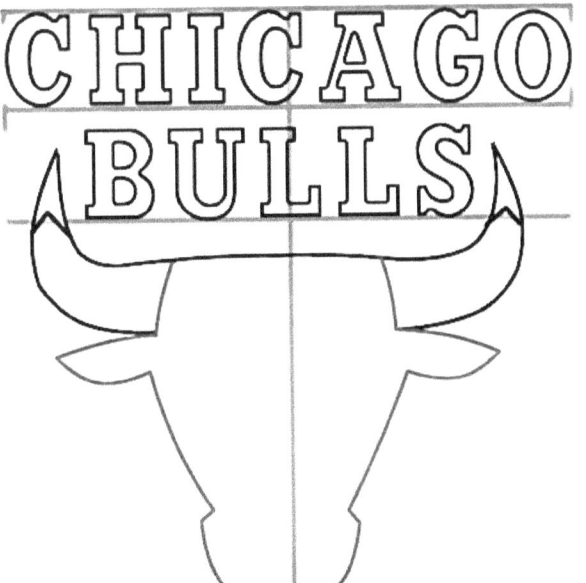

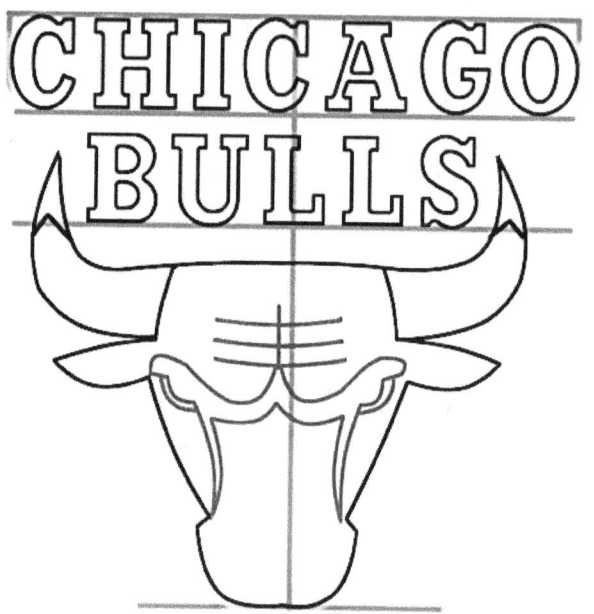
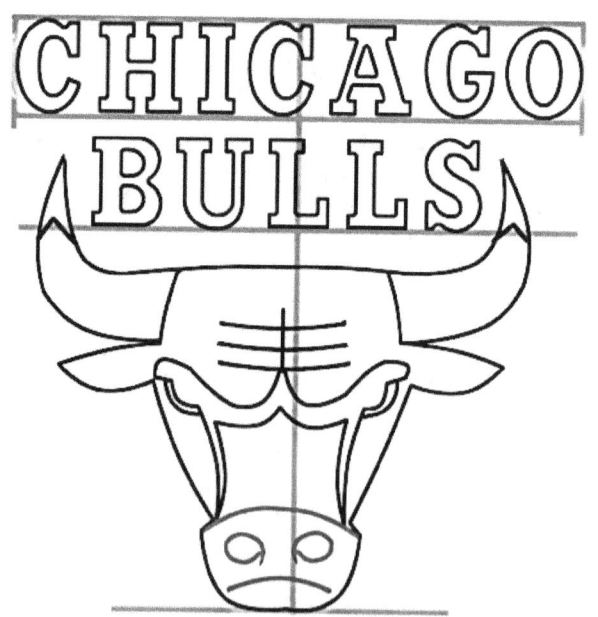

CHICAGO BULLS

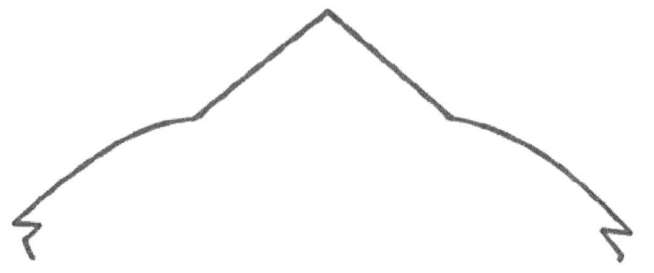
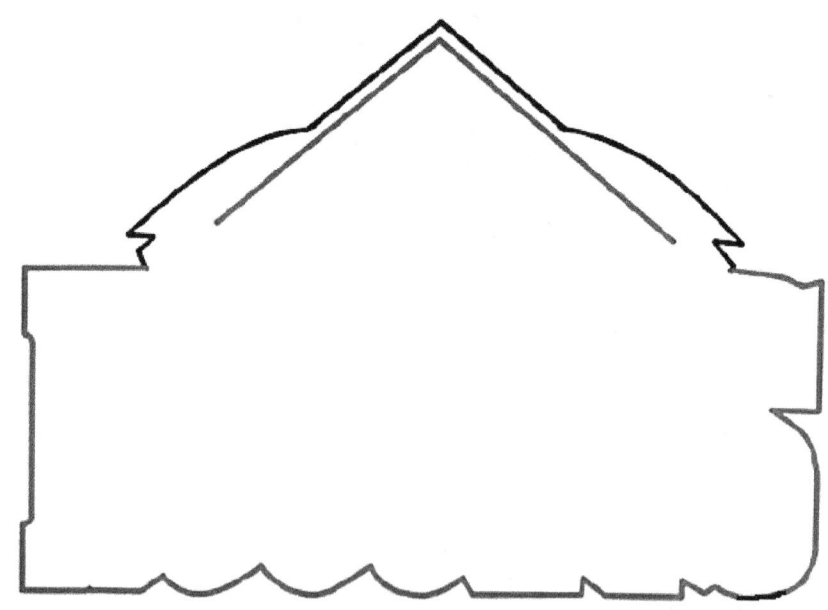

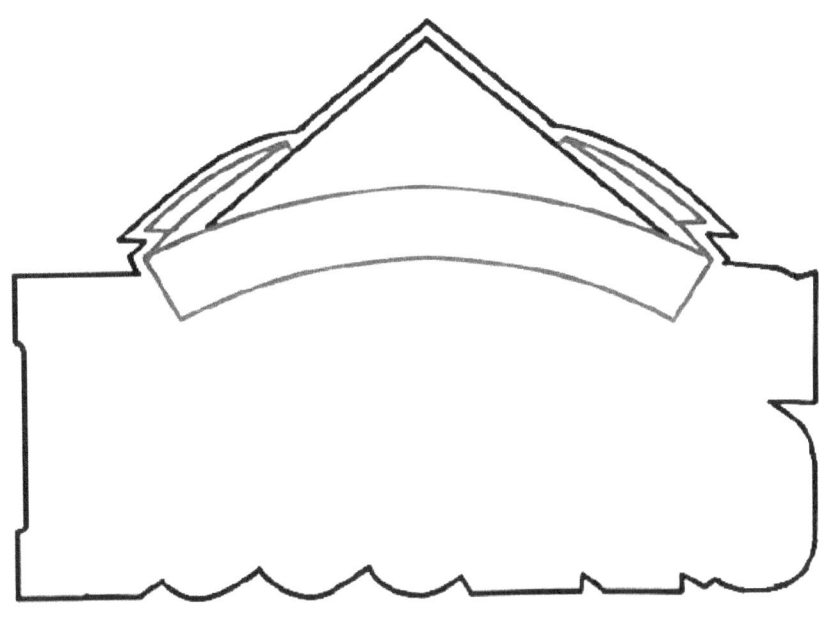
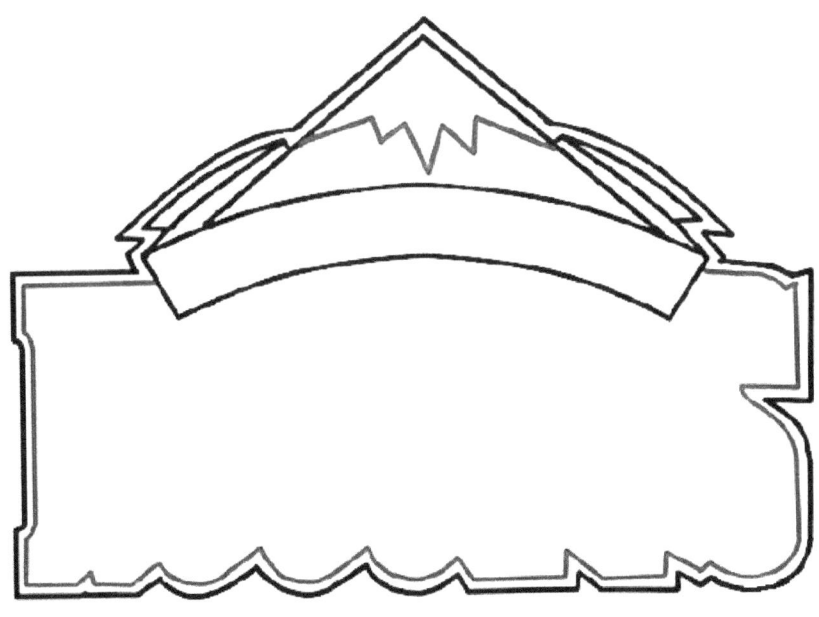

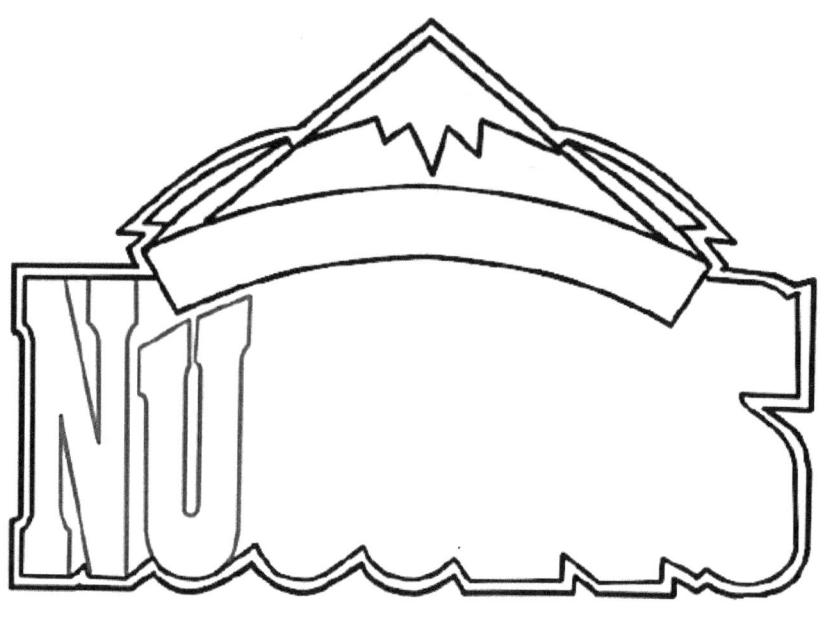
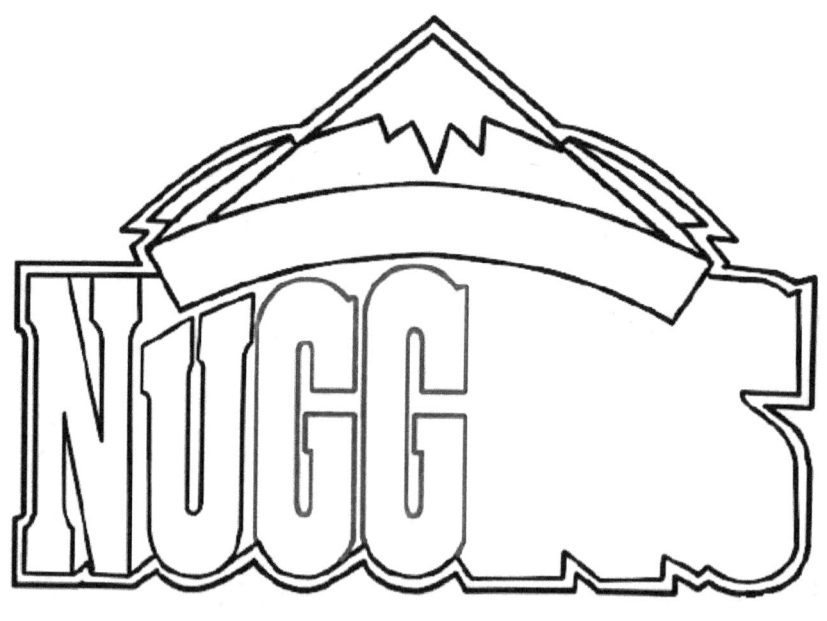

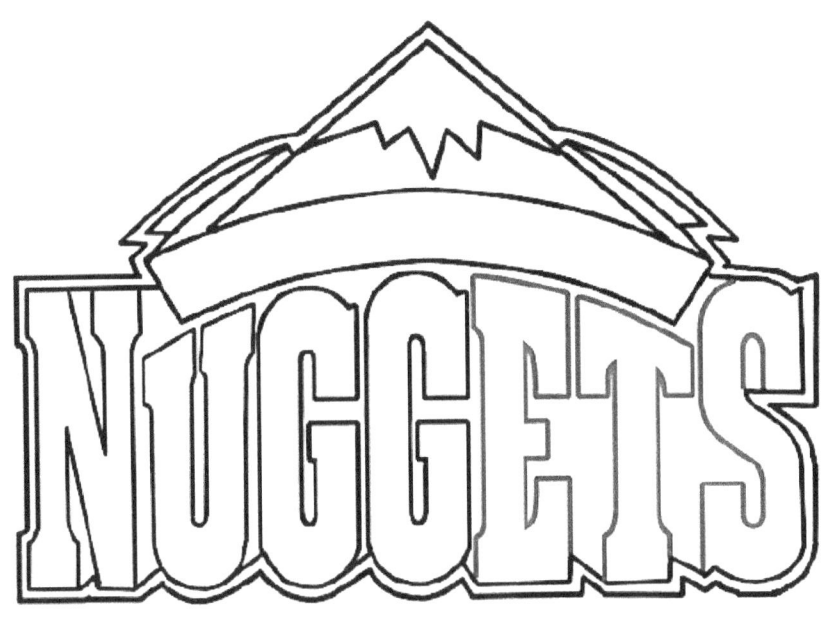
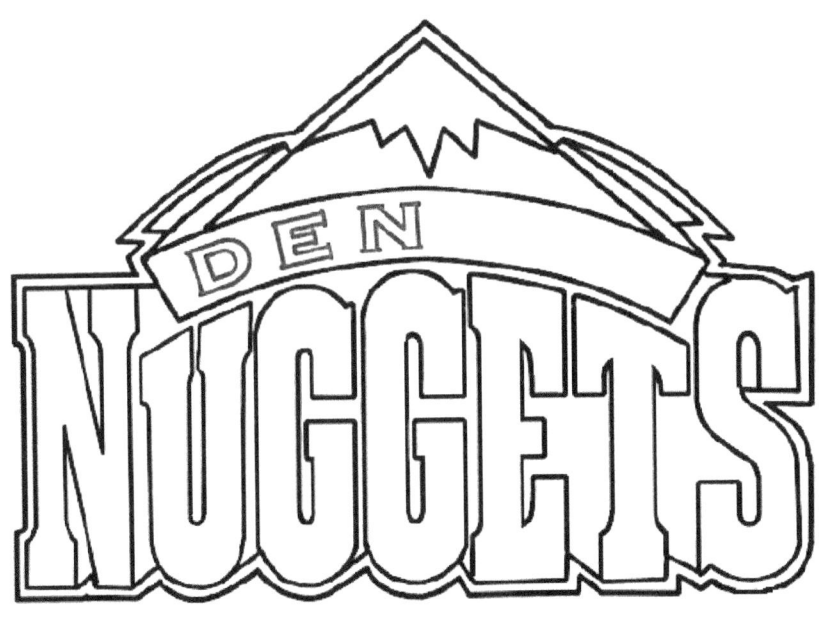

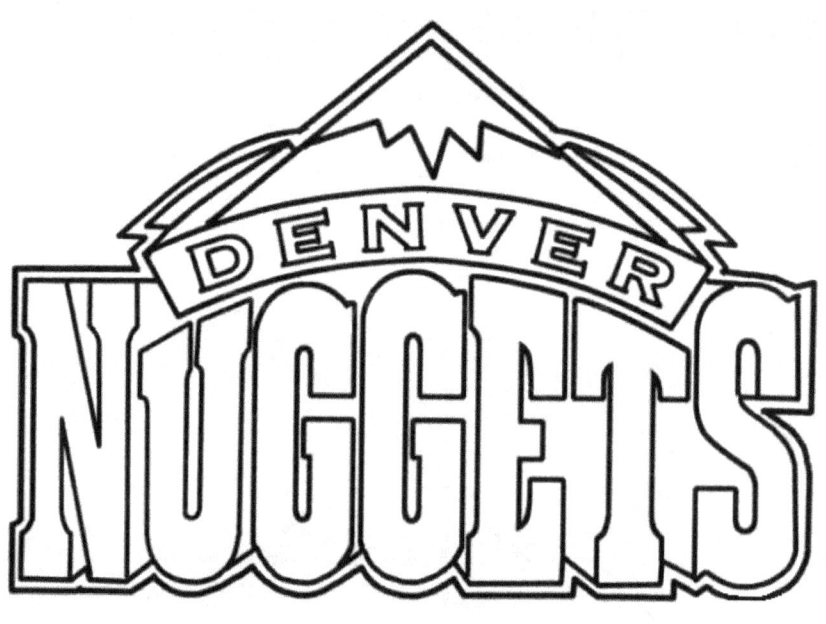

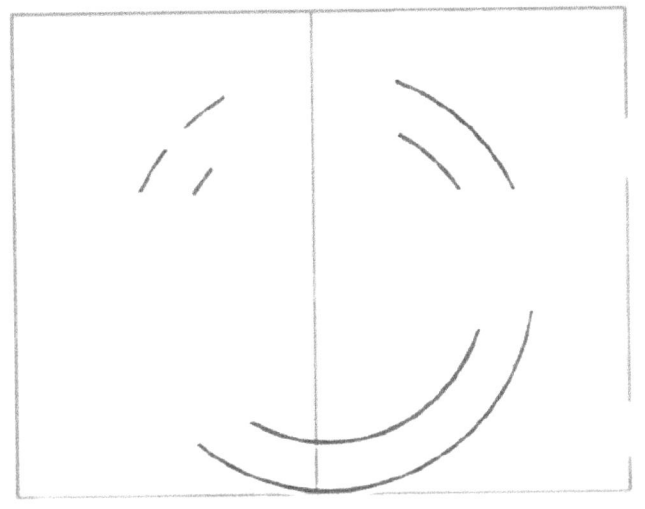

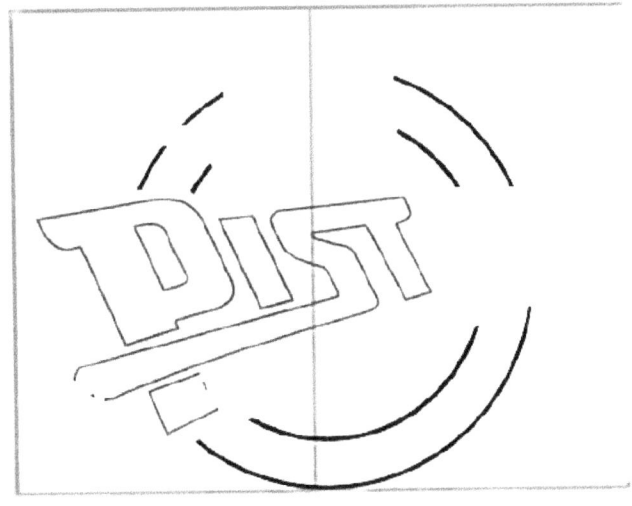

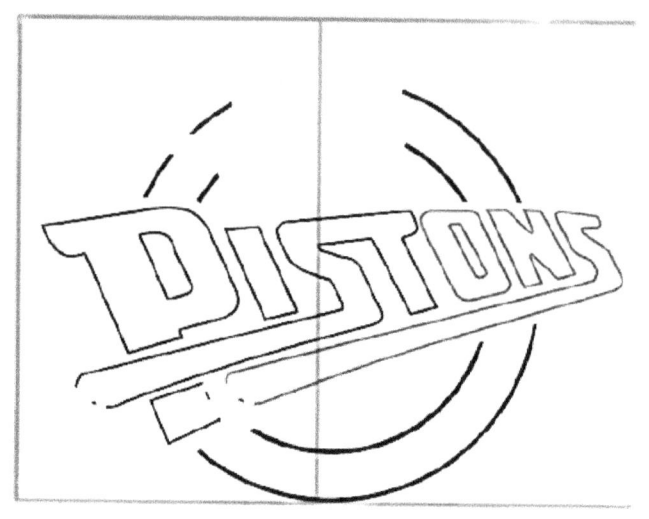

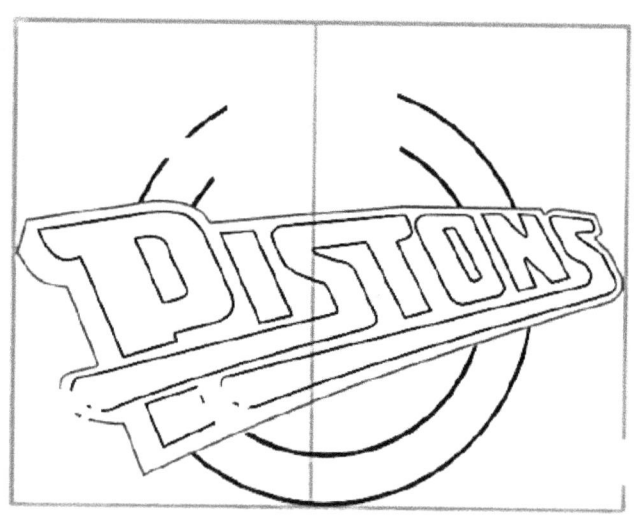

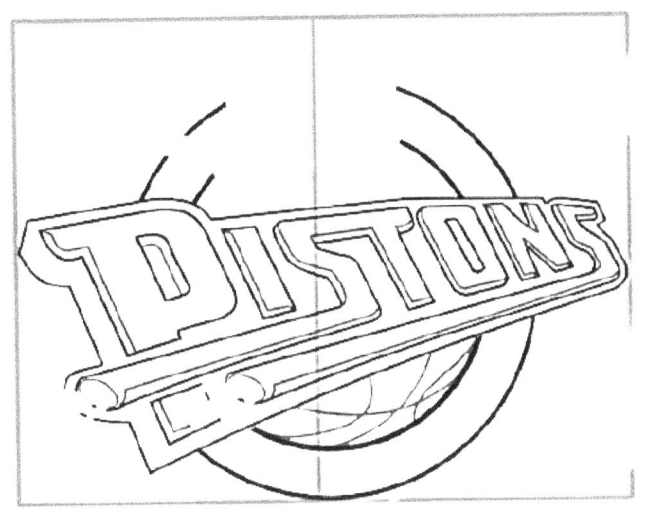

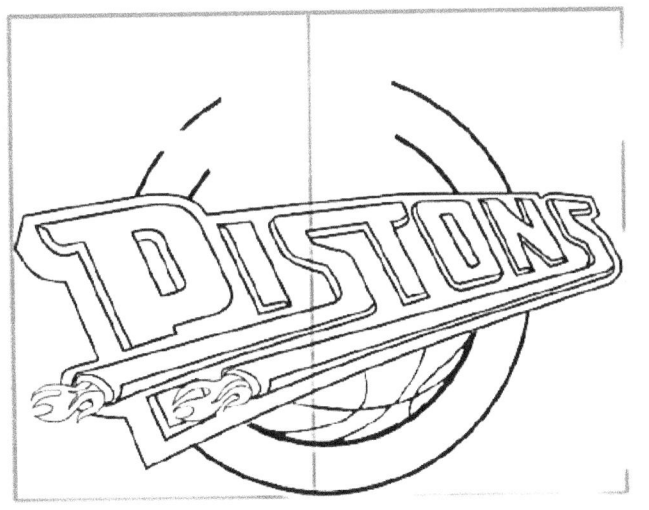

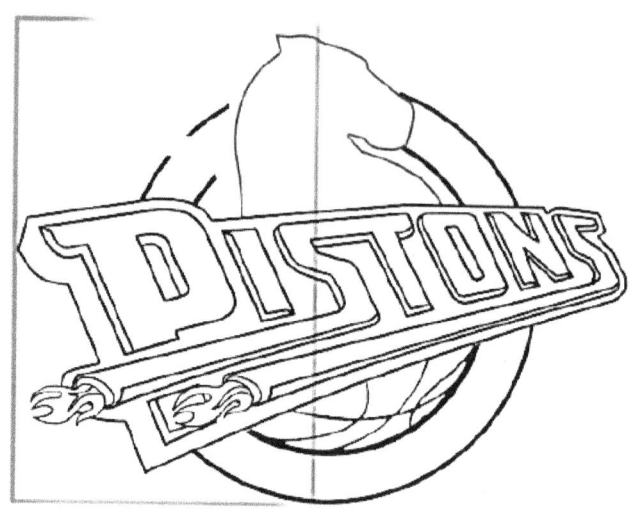
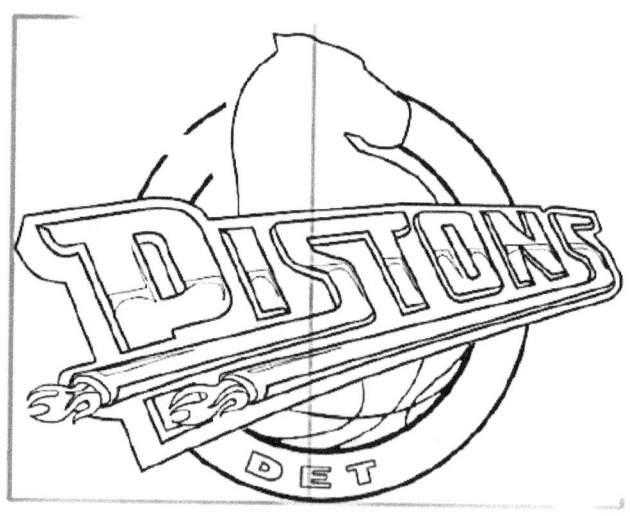

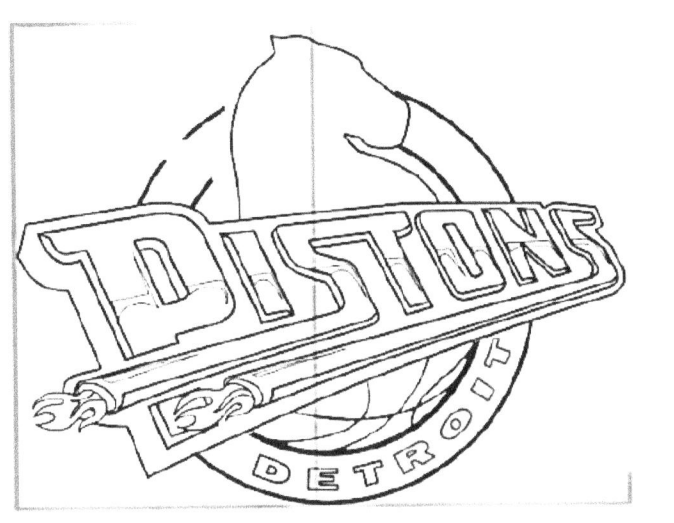

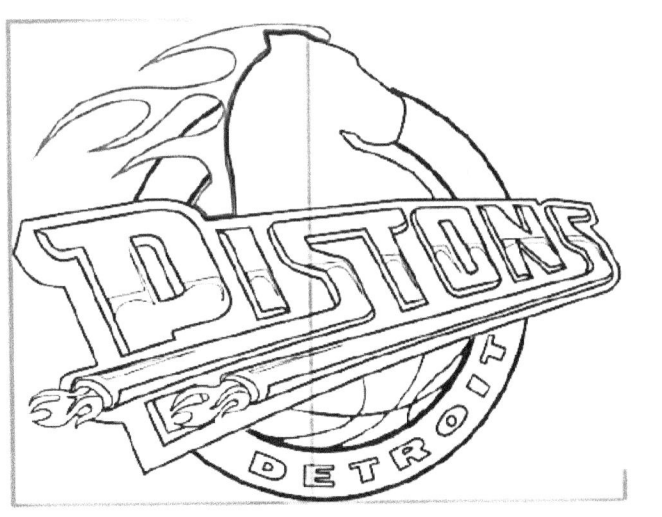

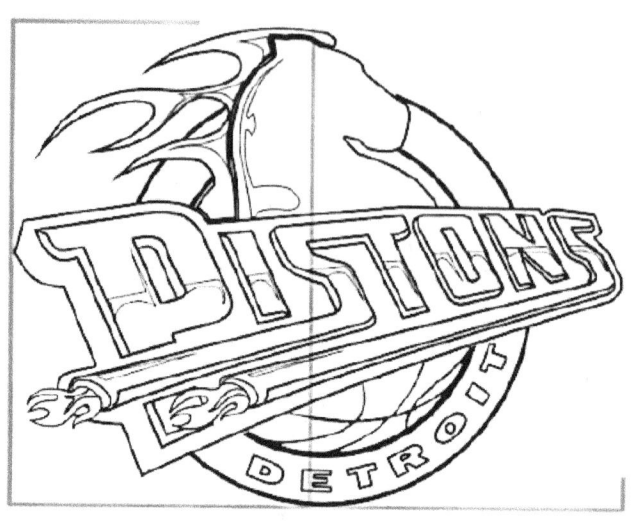

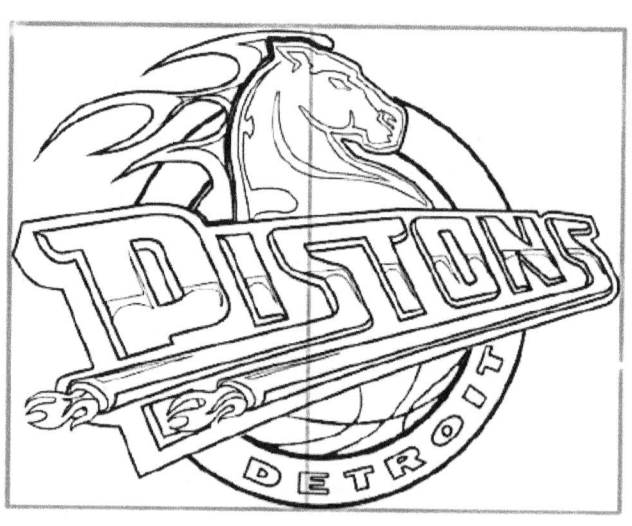

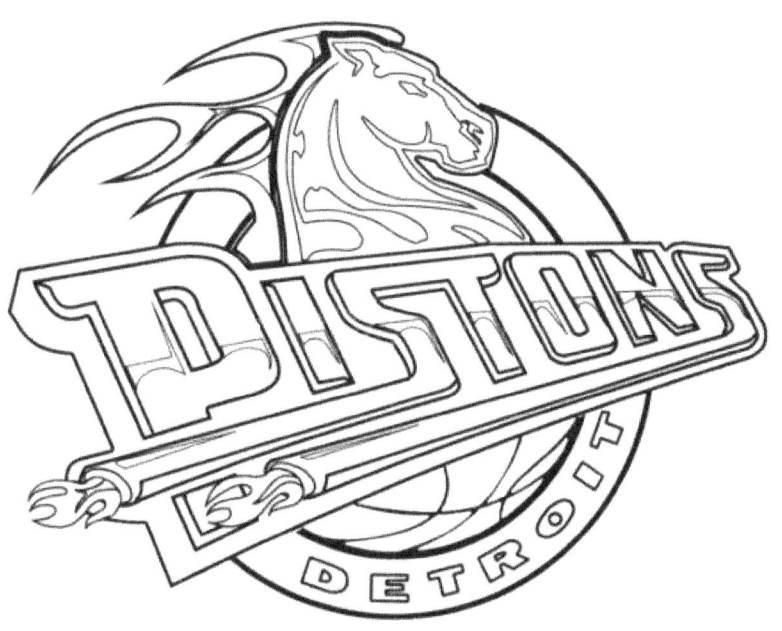

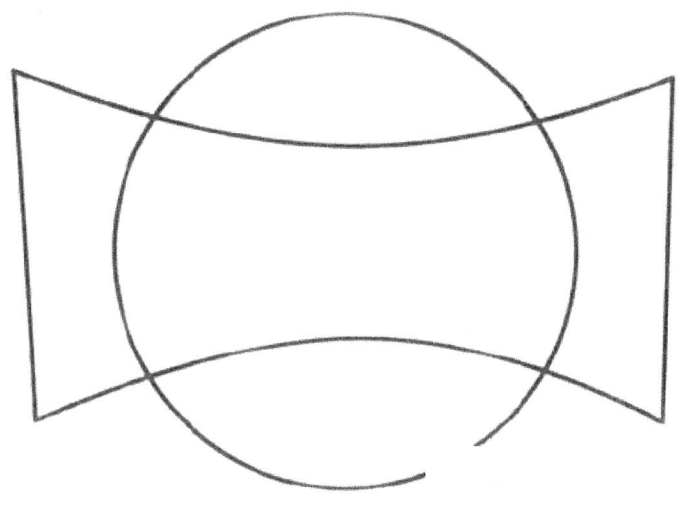

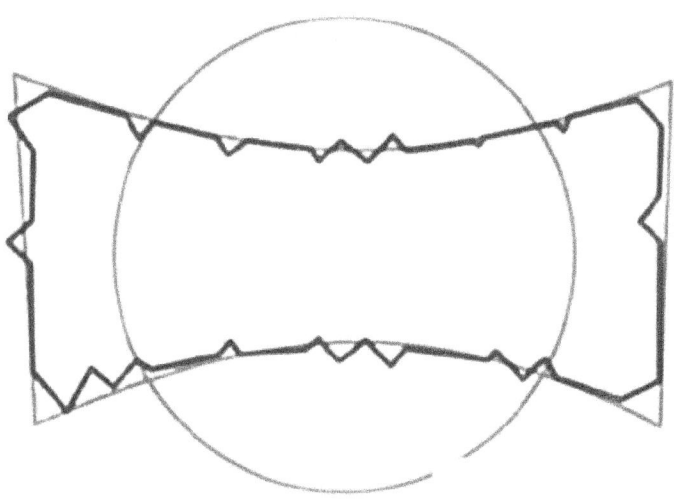

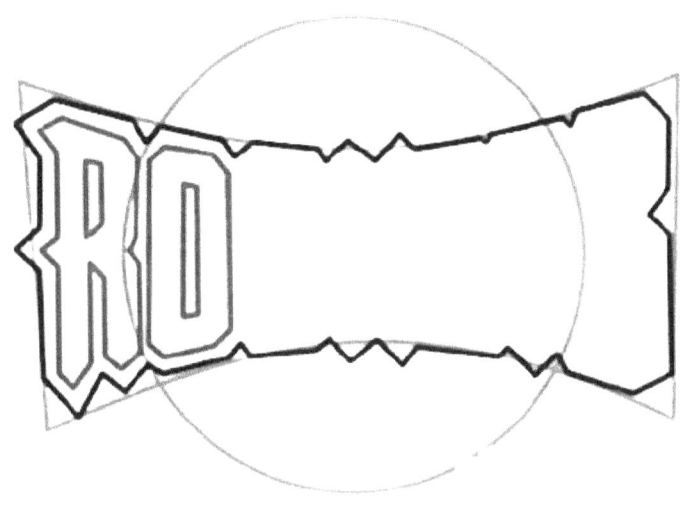

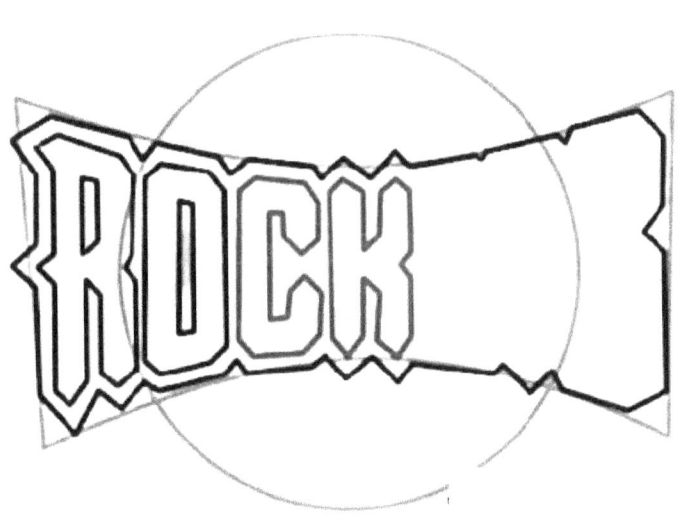

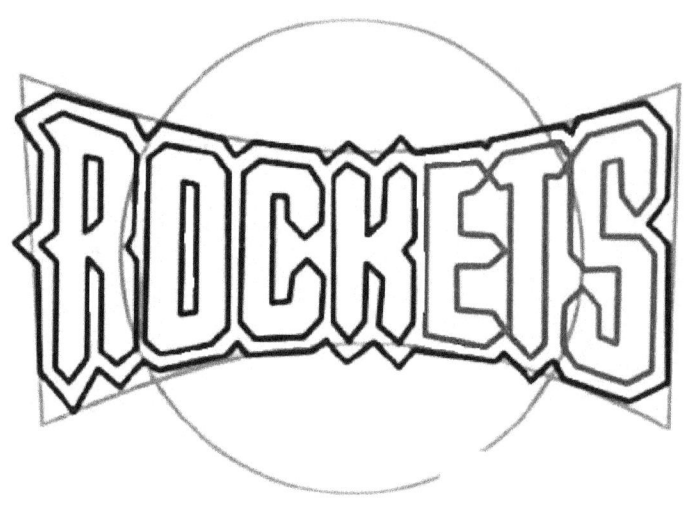
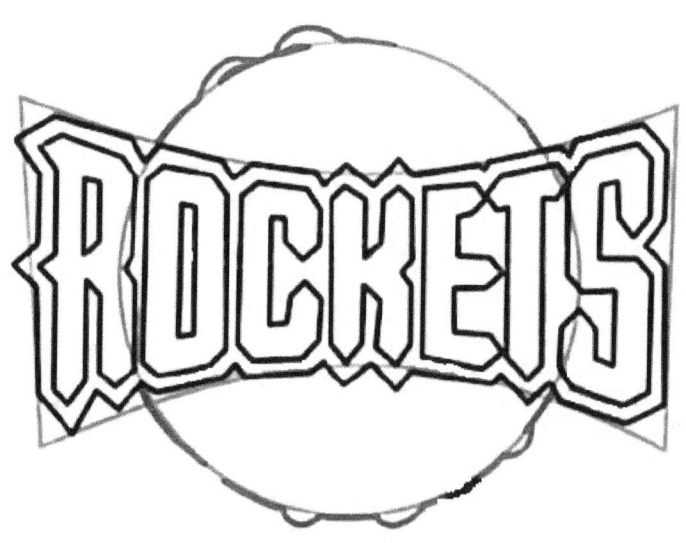

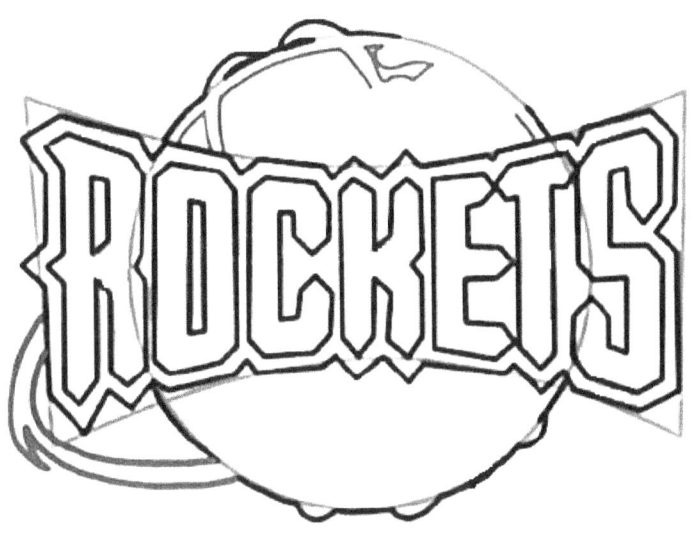
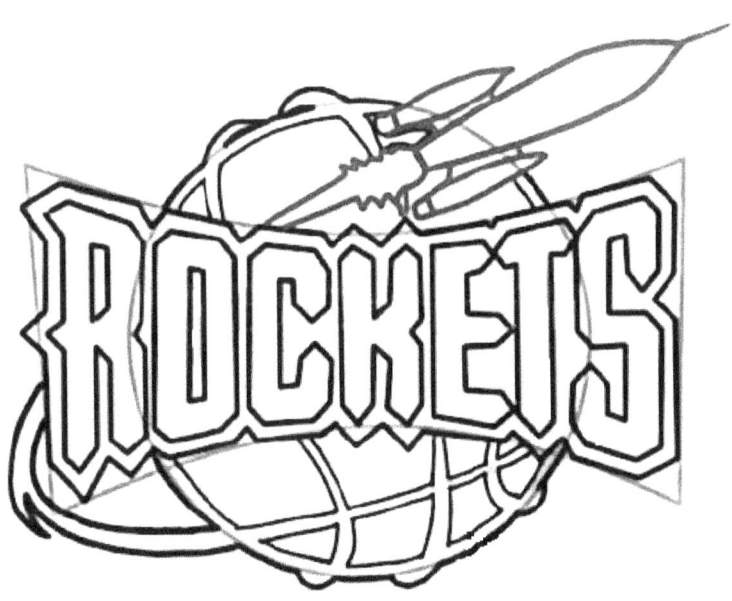

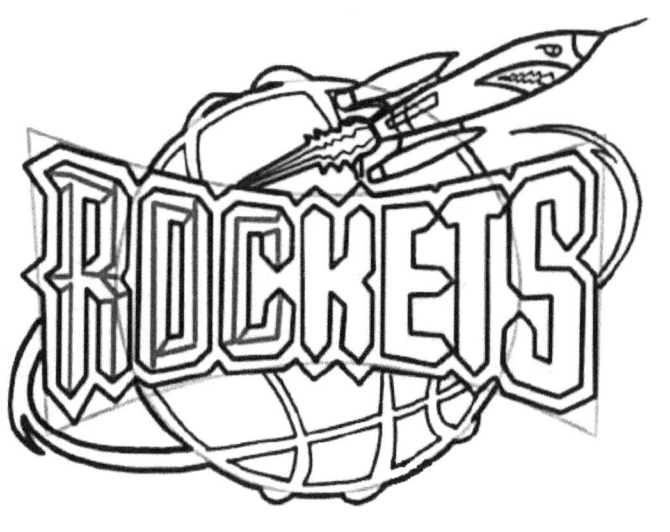

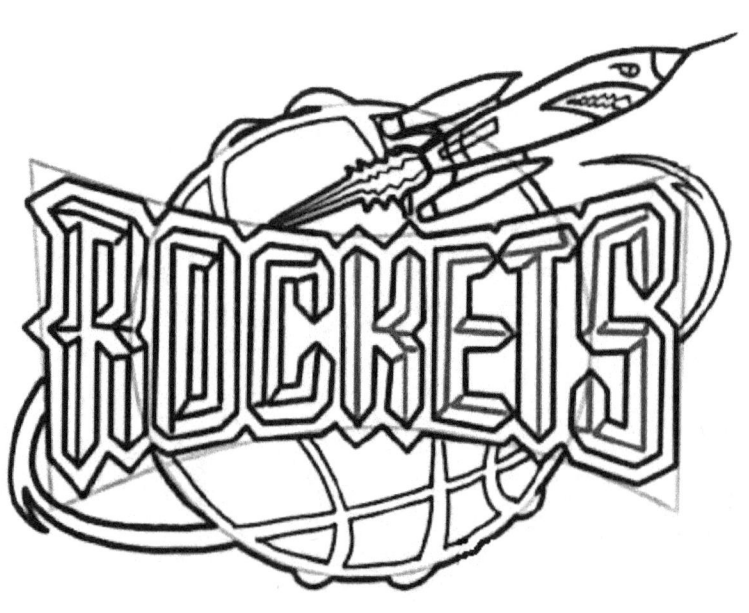

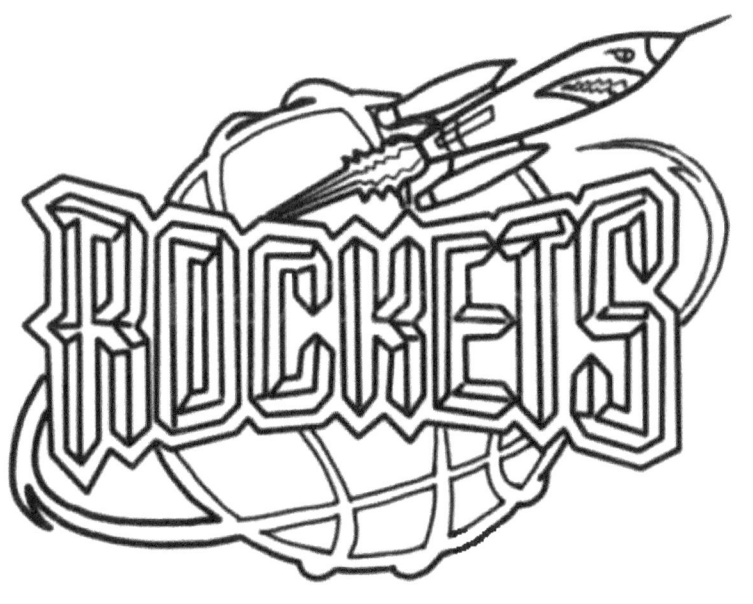

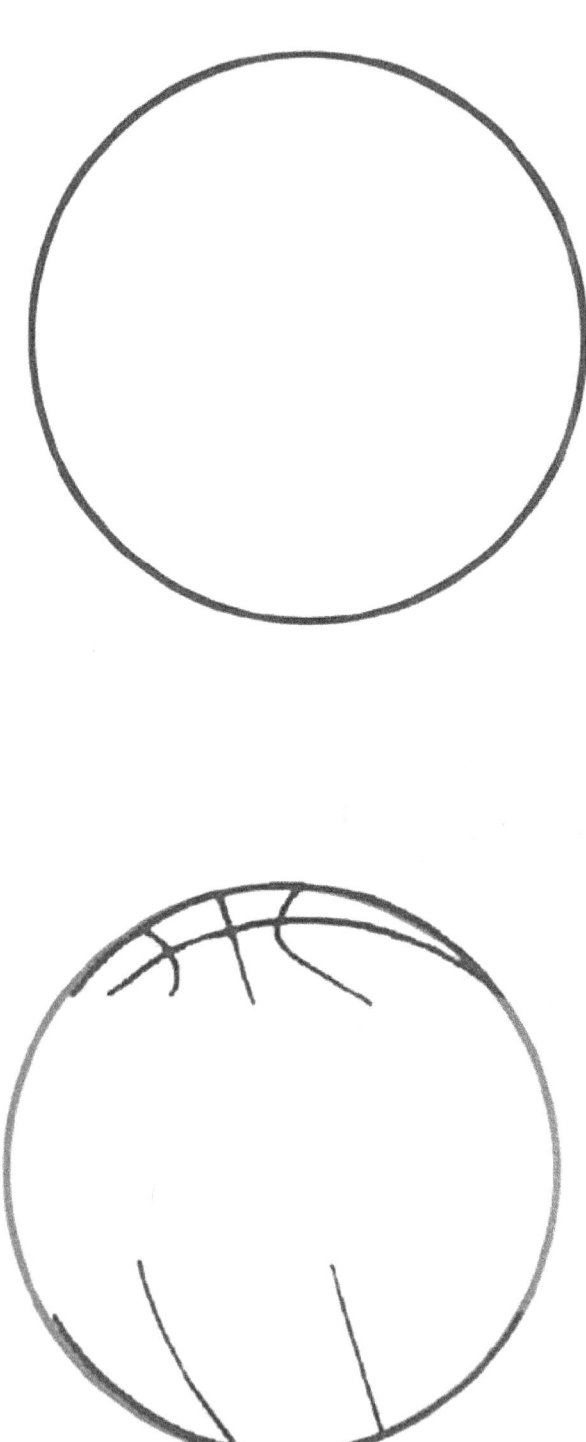

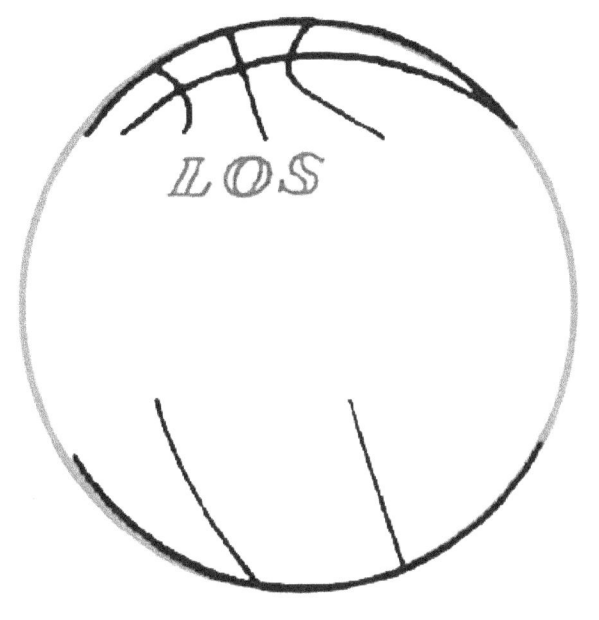

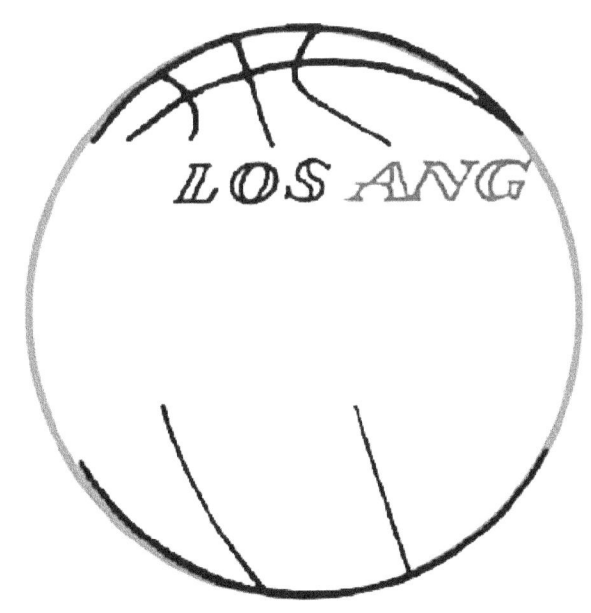

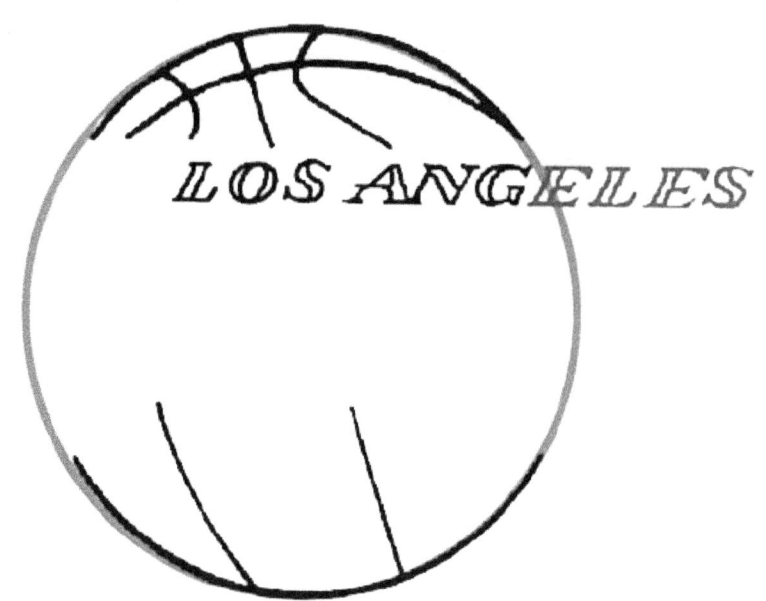
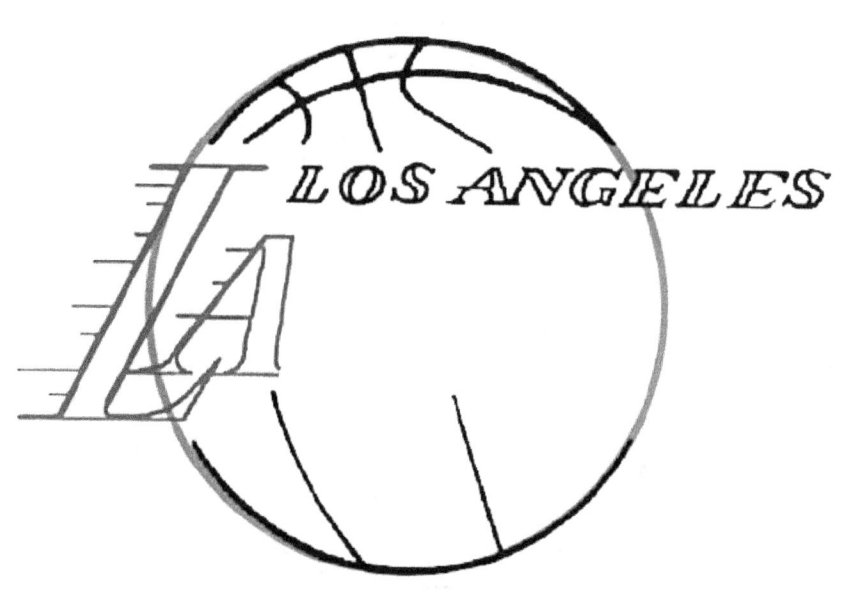

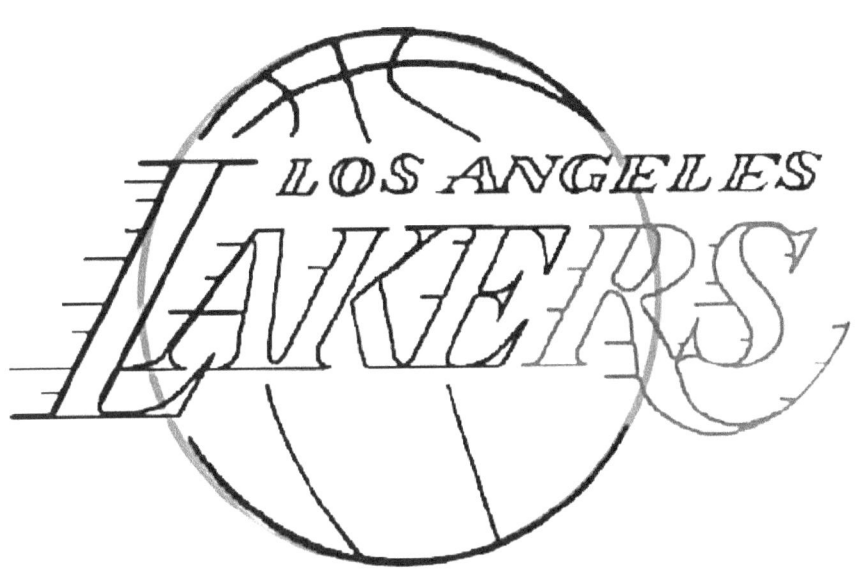
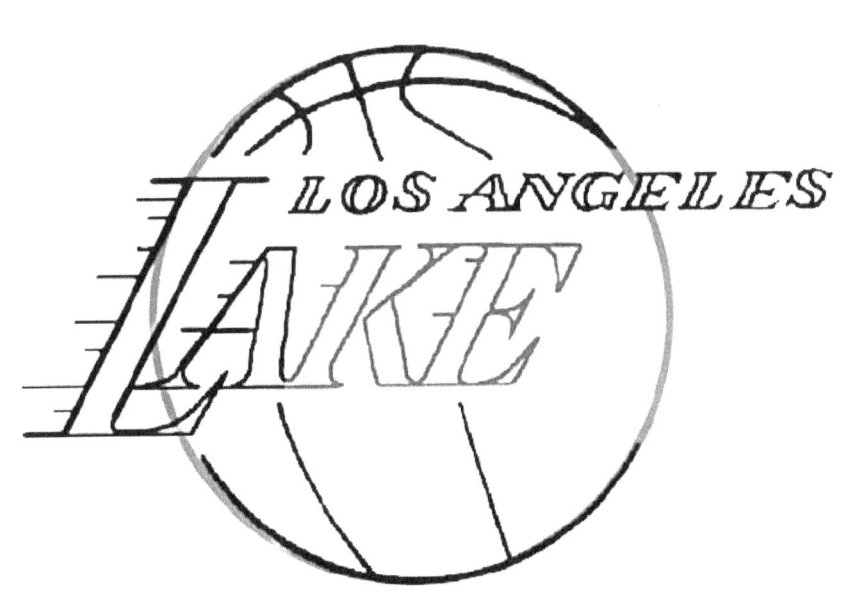

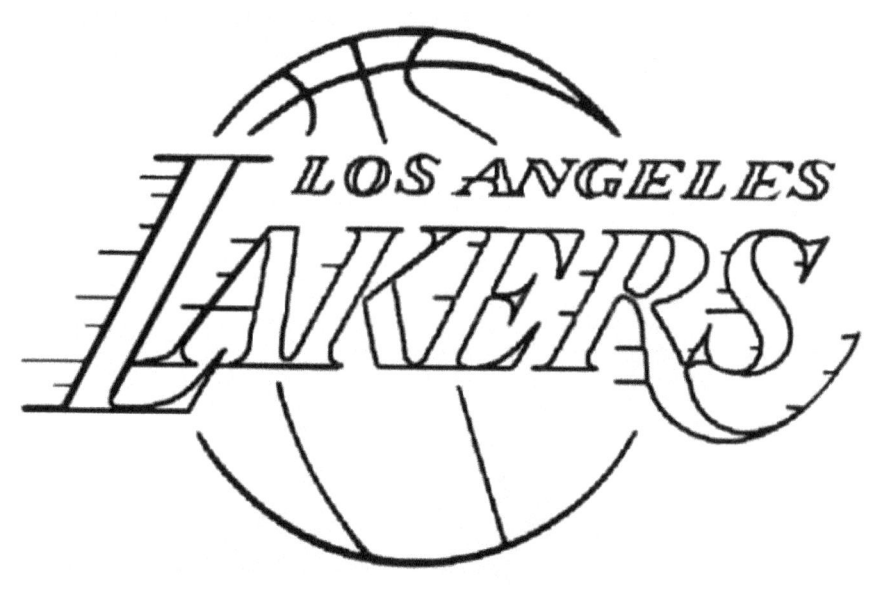

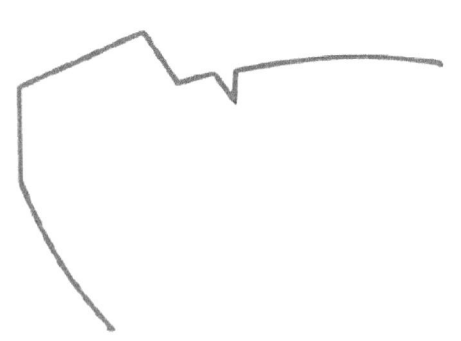

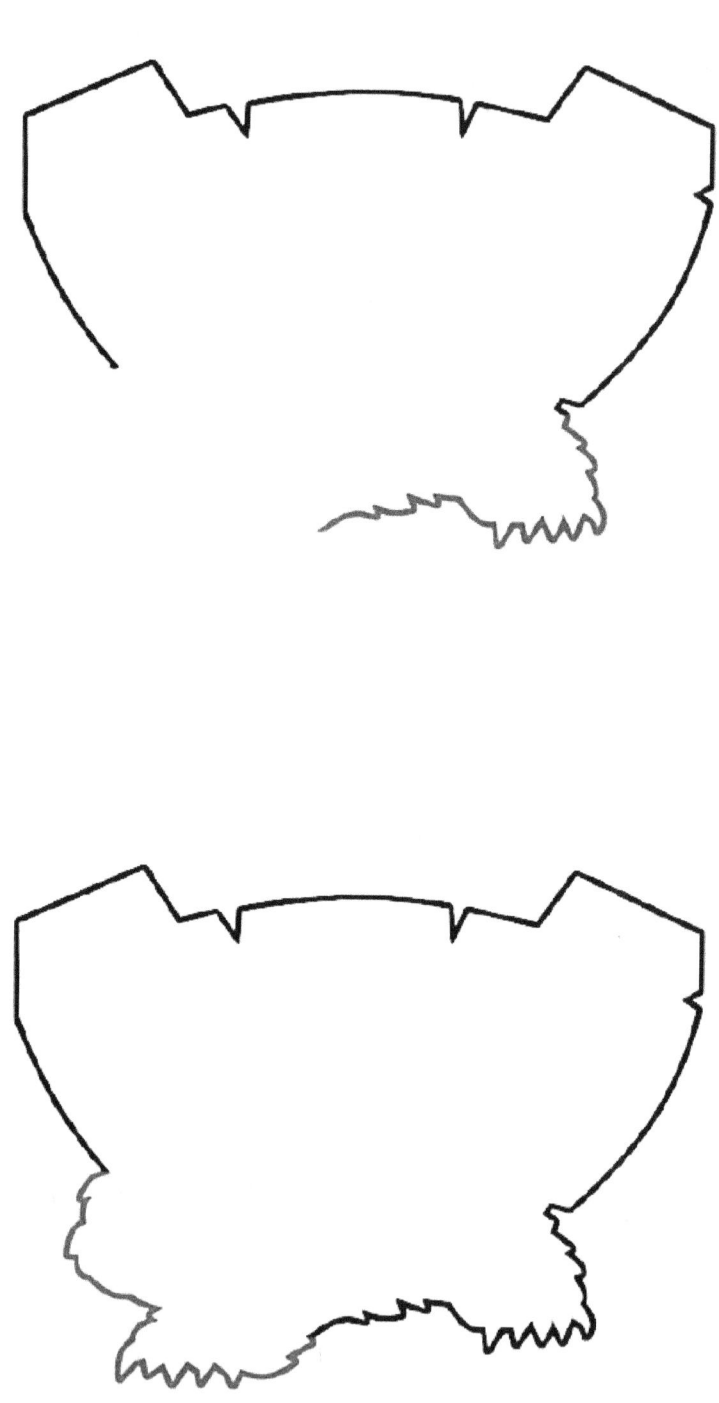

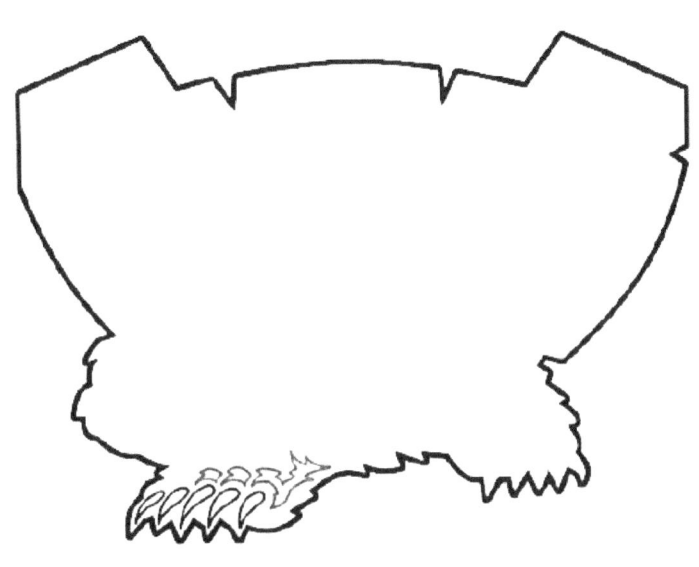

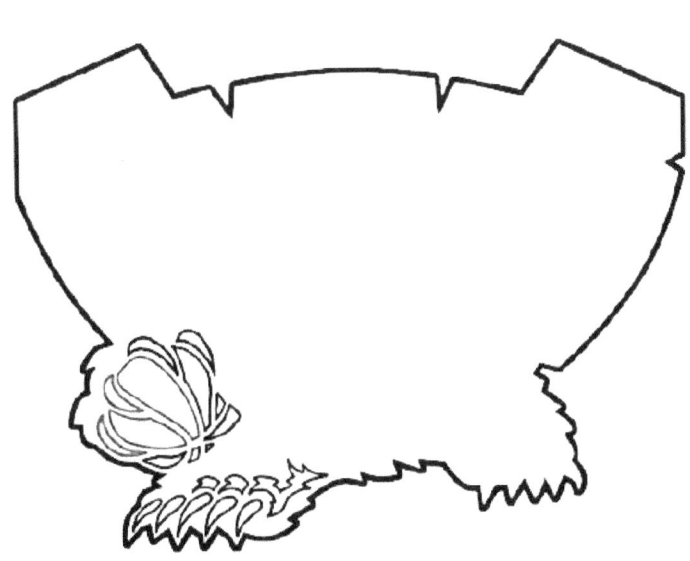

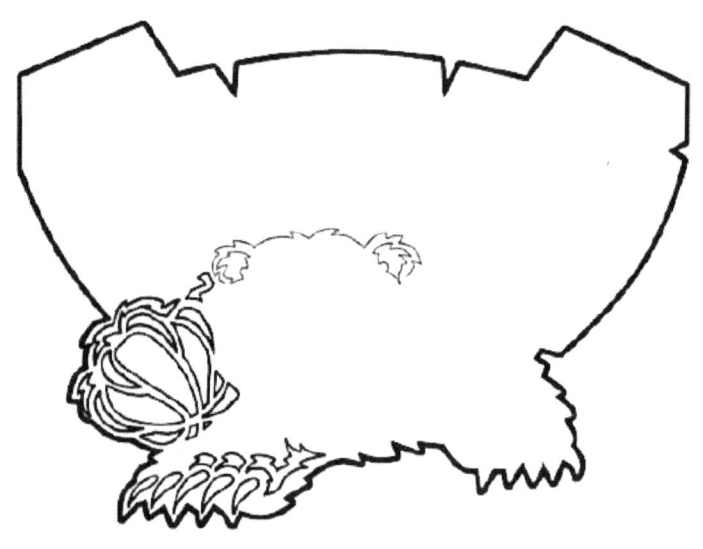
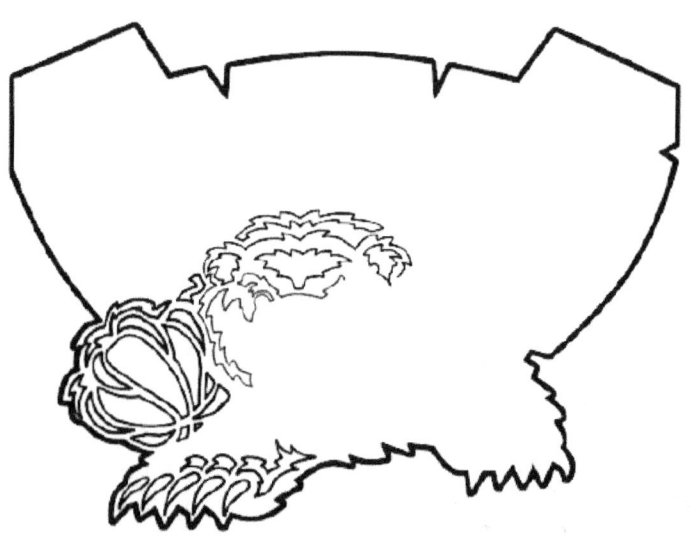

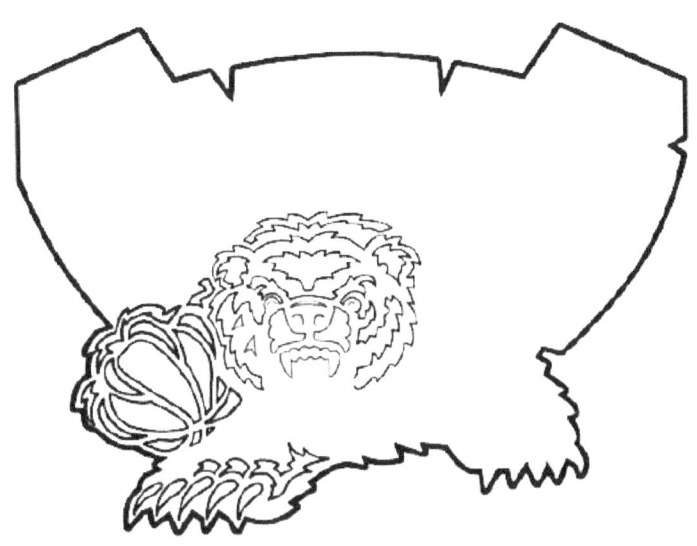
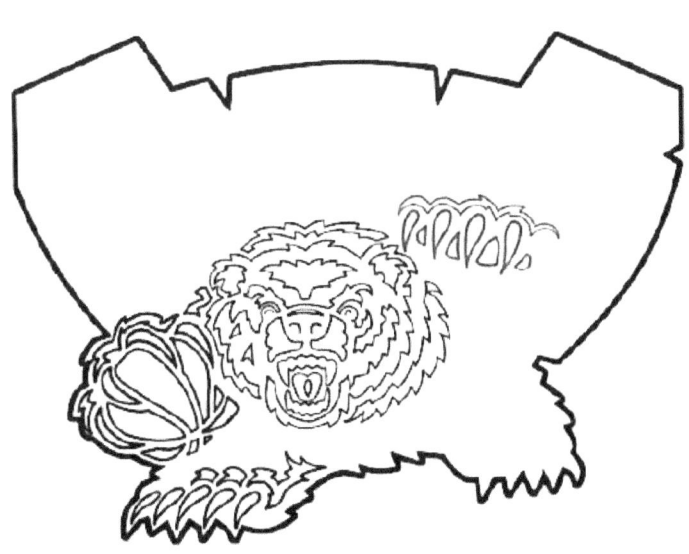

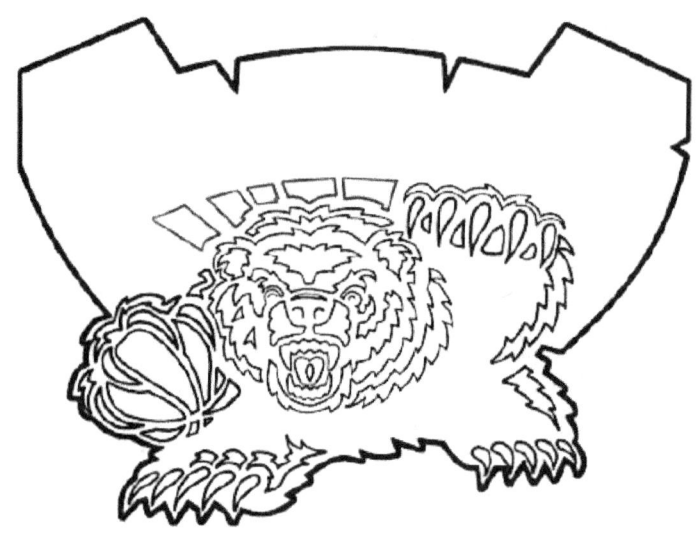

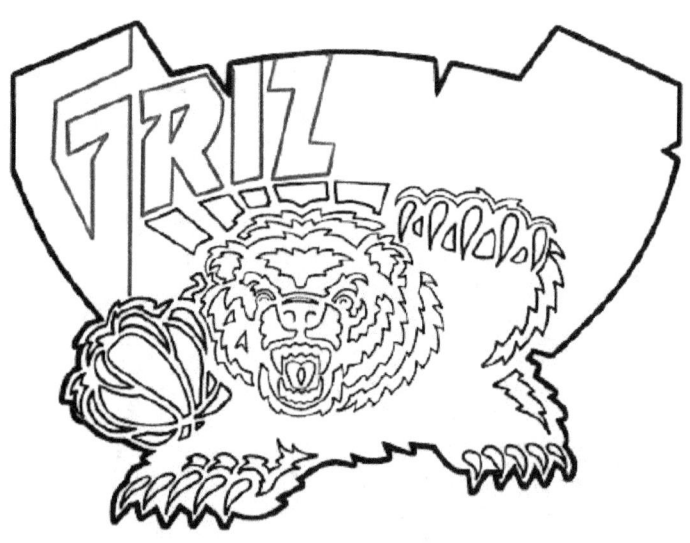

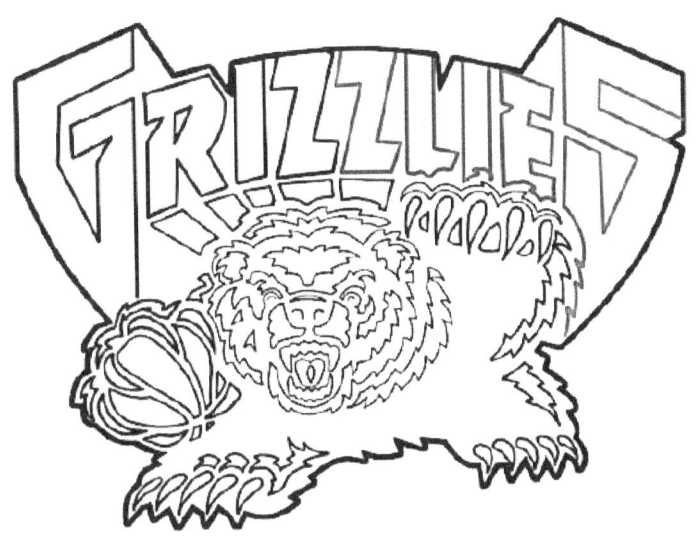

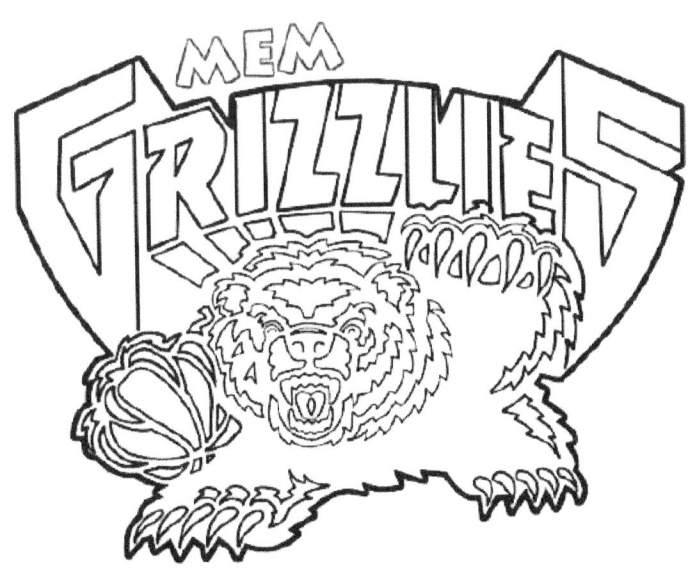

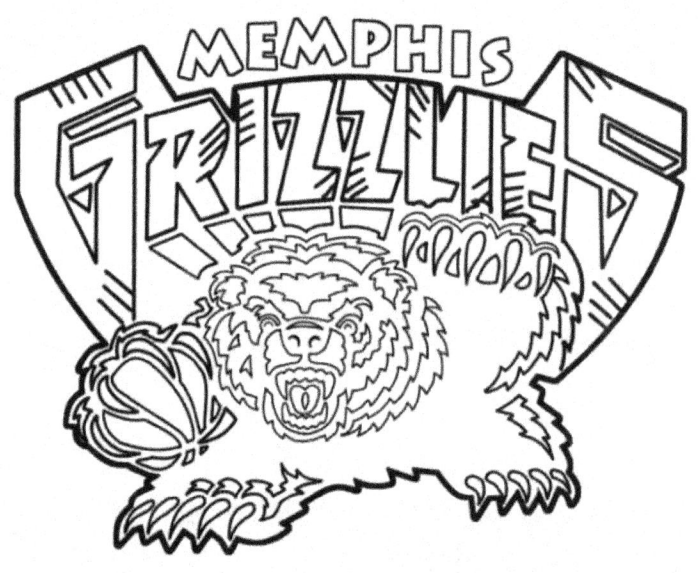

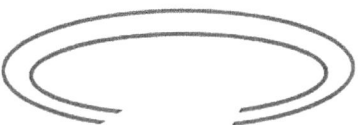

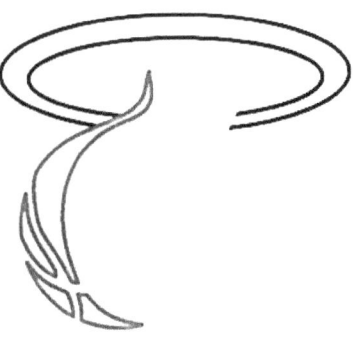

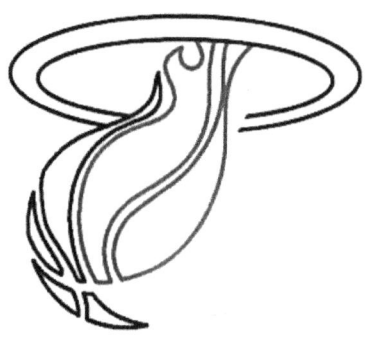

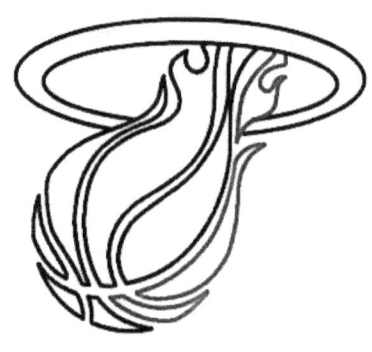

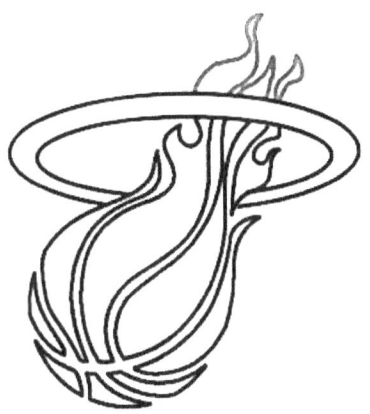

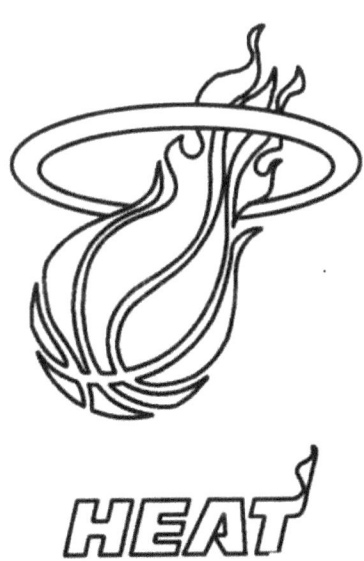

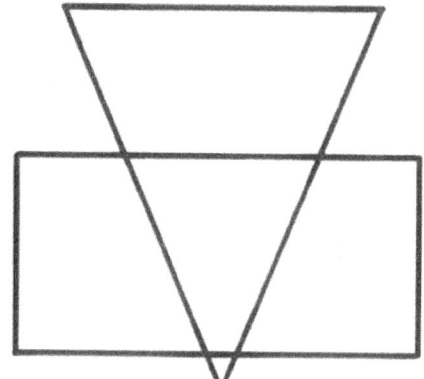

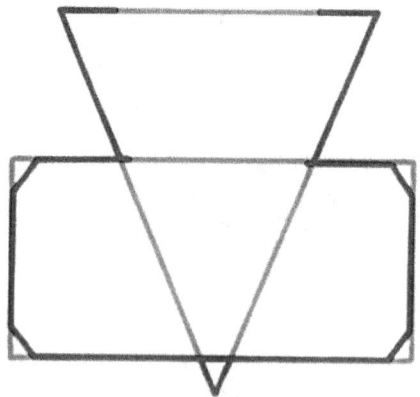

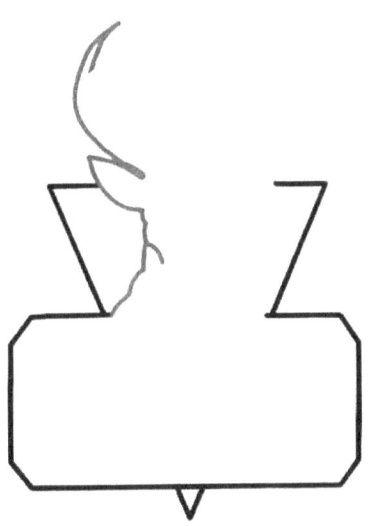

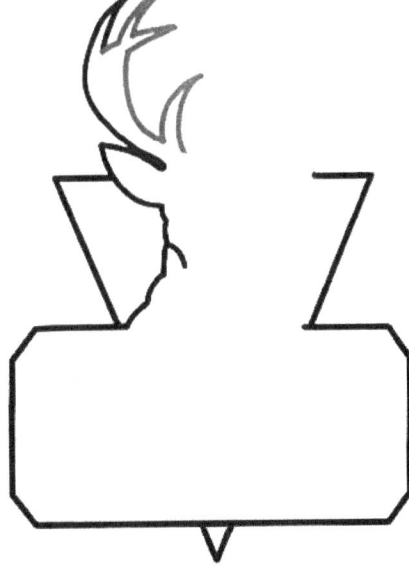

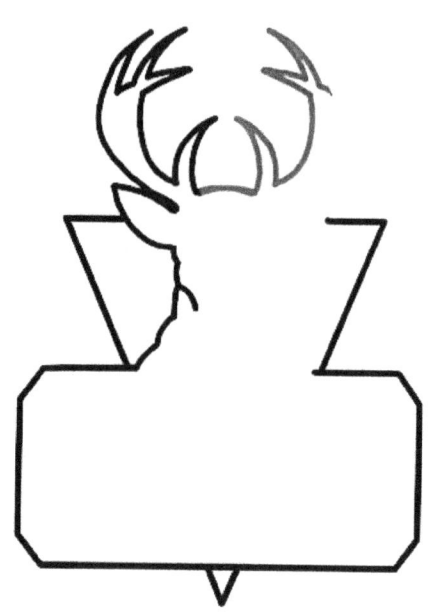
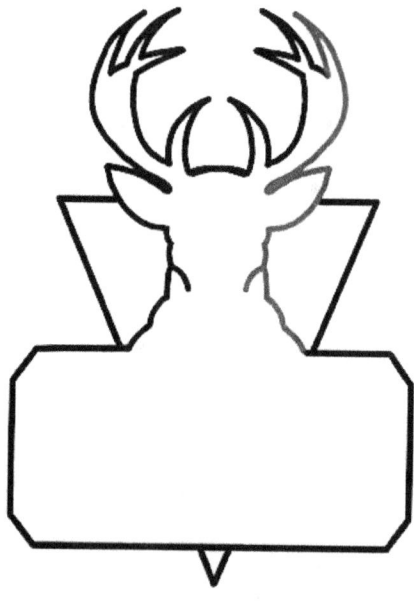

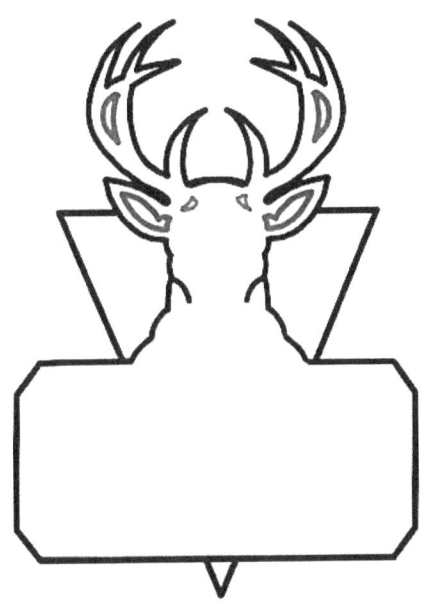
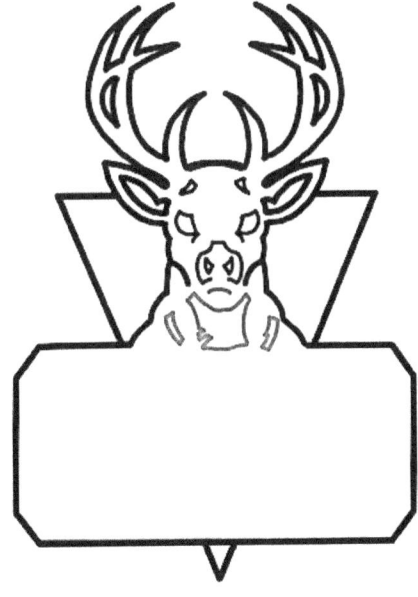

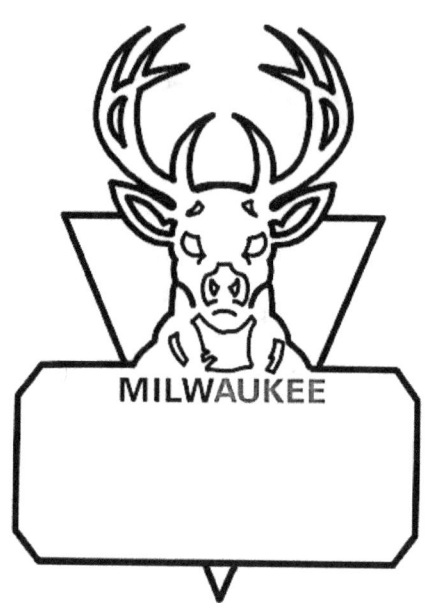

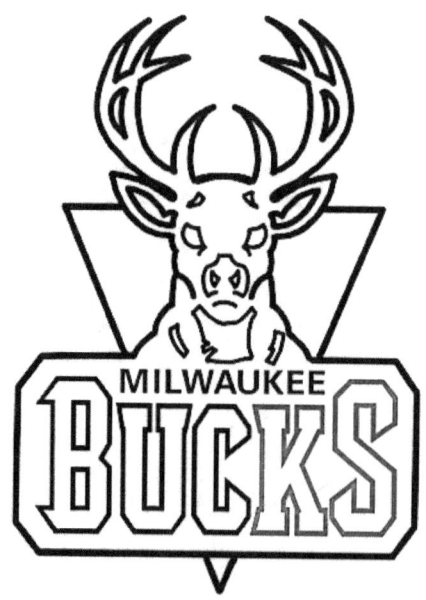

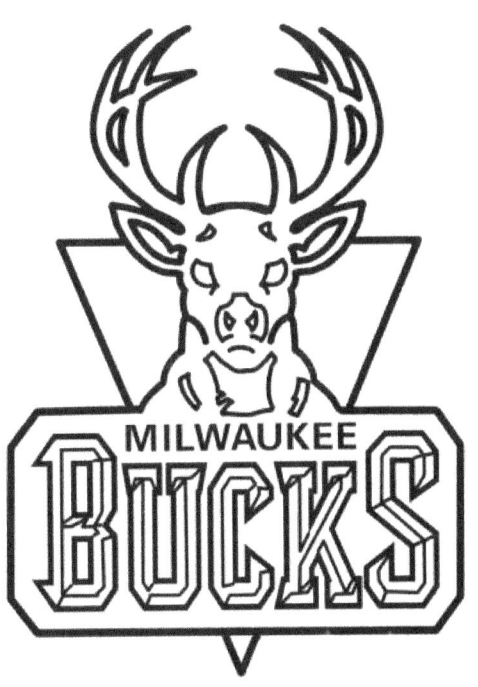

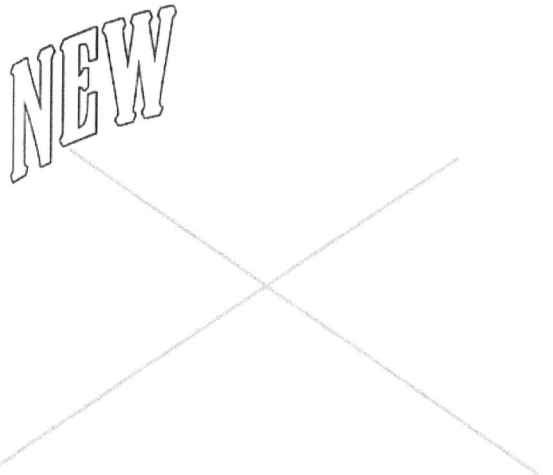

NEW ORLEANS

NEW ORLEANS

HOR

NEW ORLEANS

HORNETS

NEW ORLEANS

HORNETS

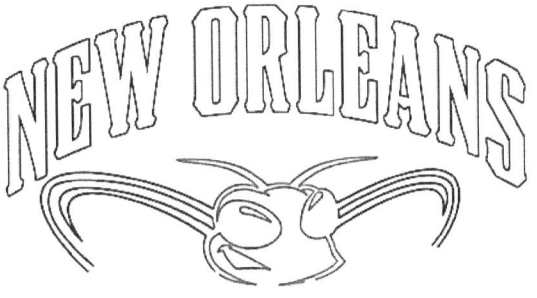

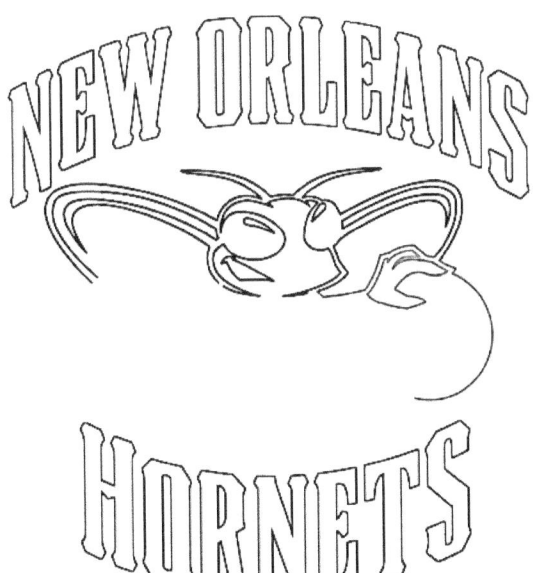

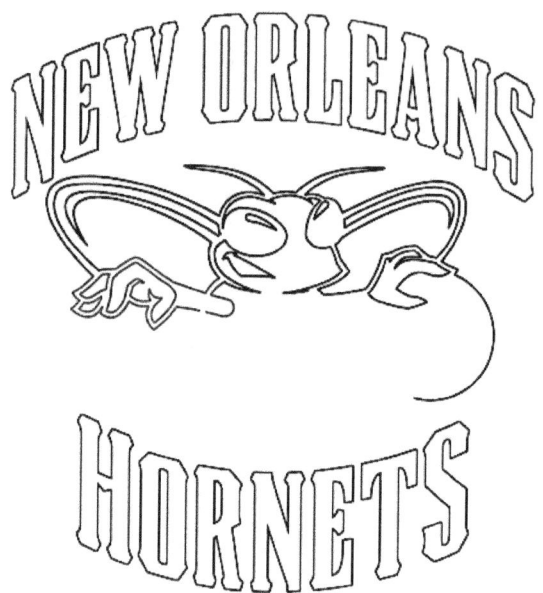
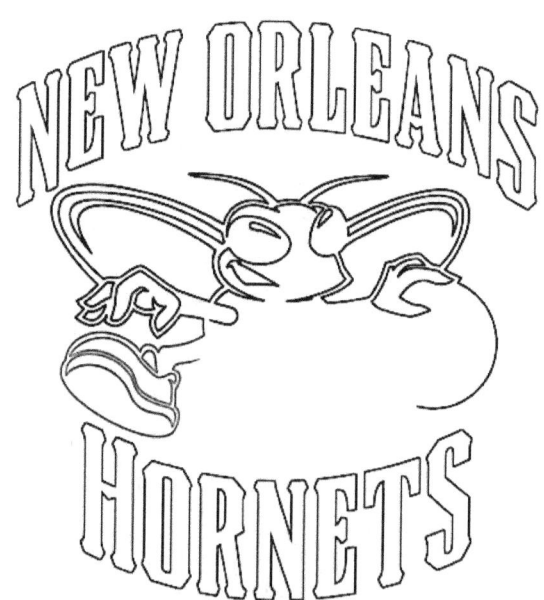

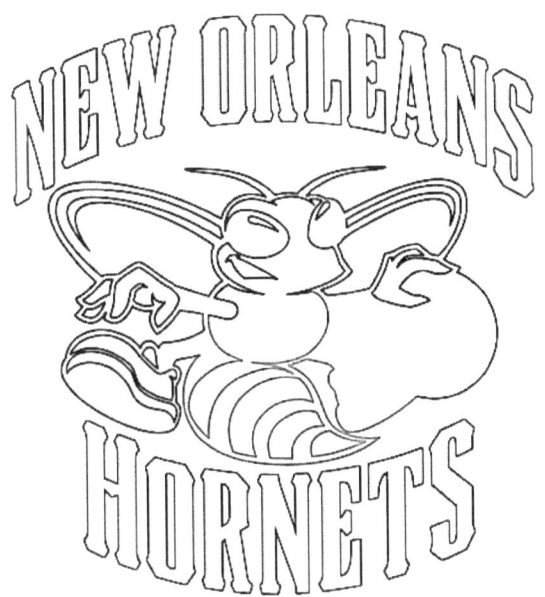

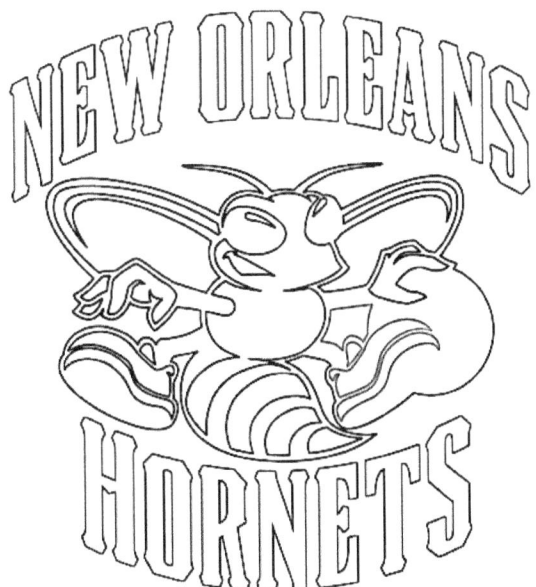

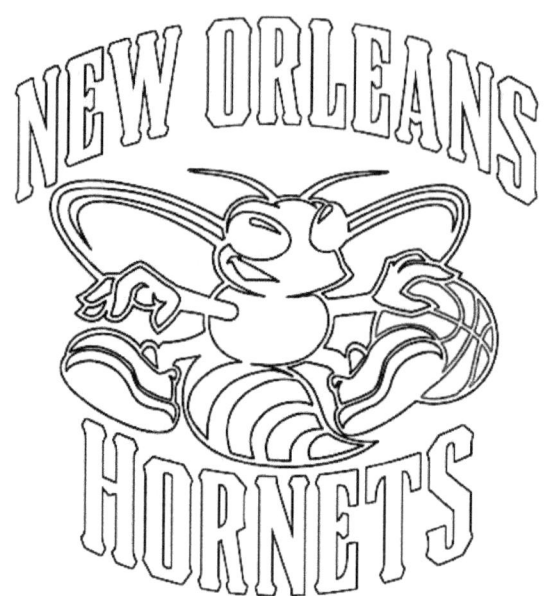
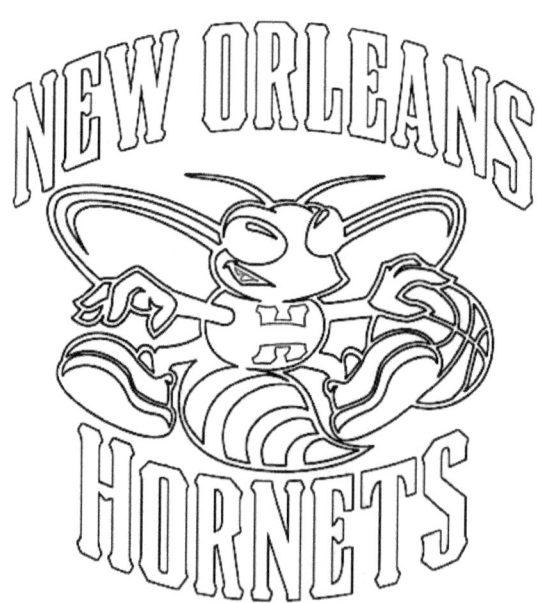

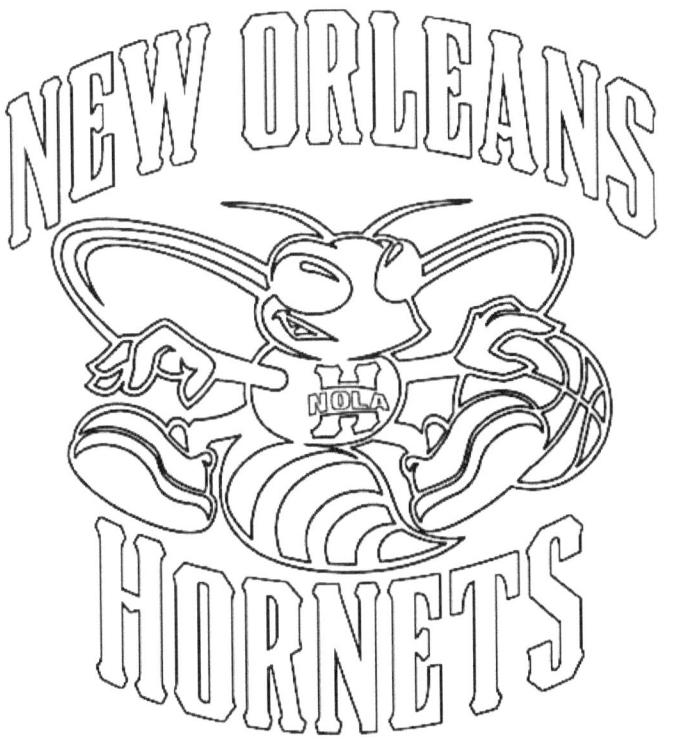

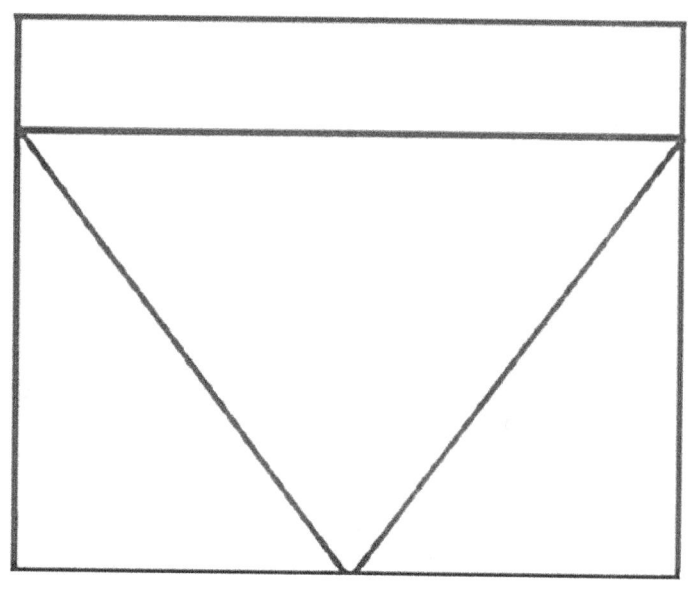

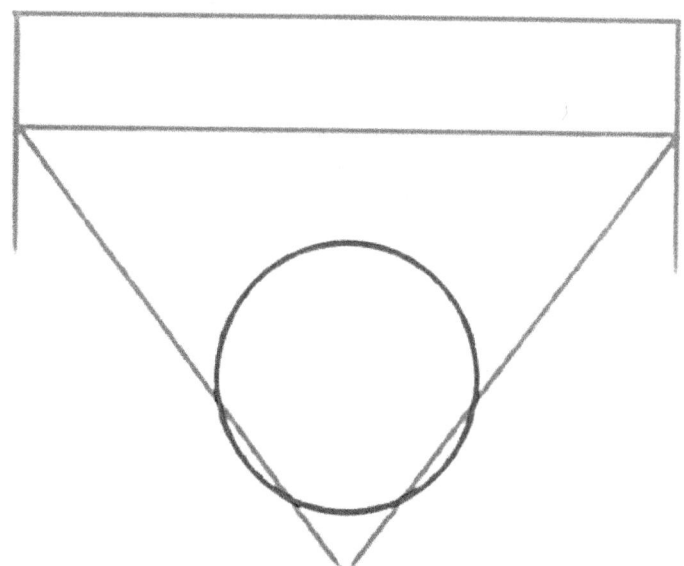

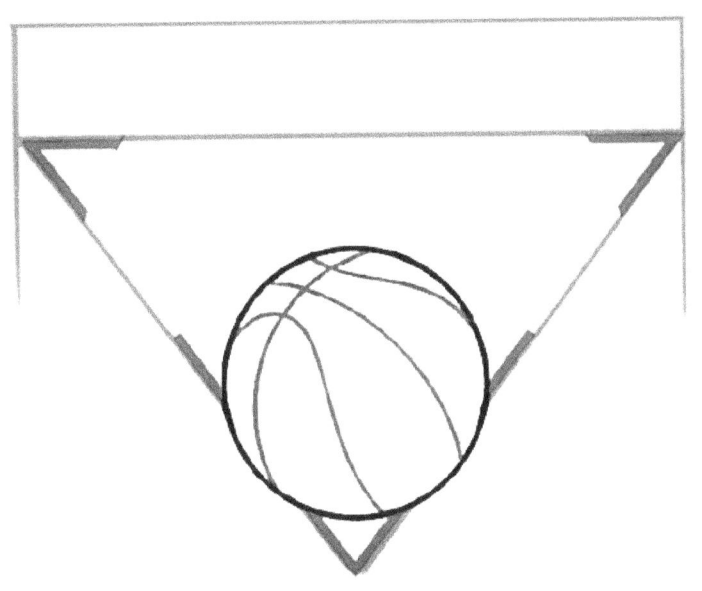

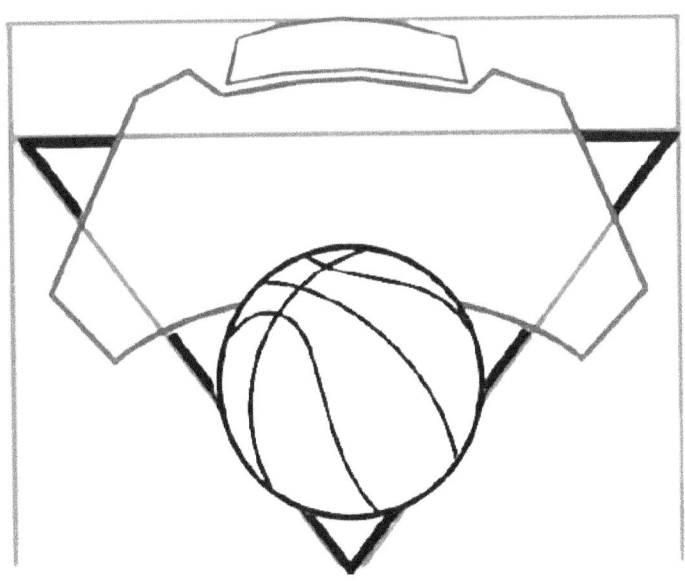

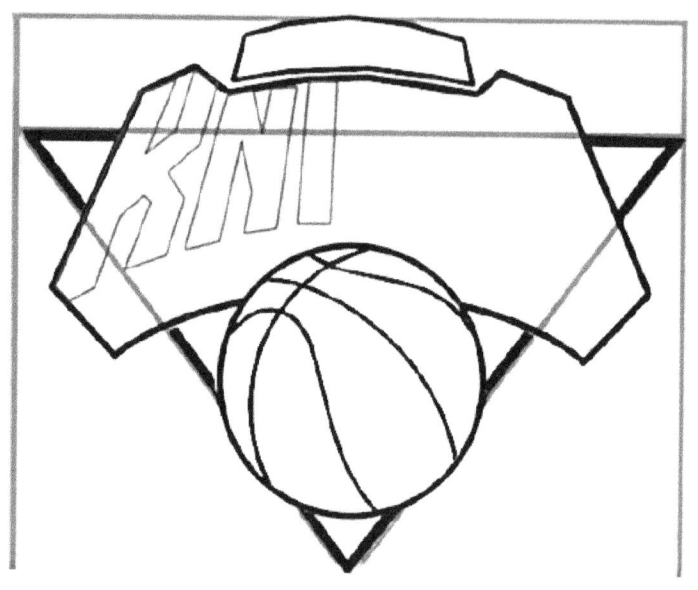
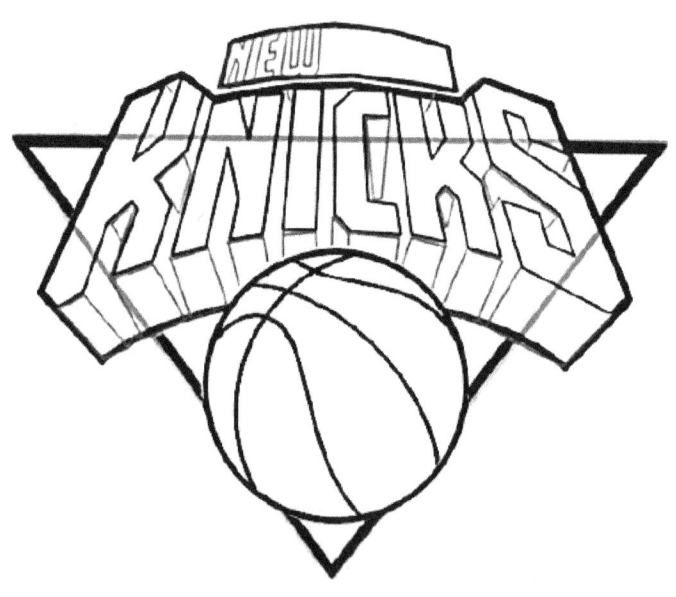

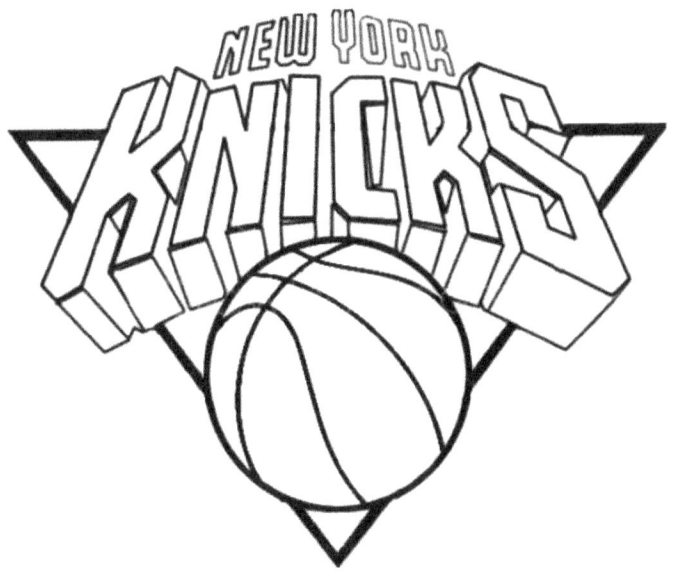

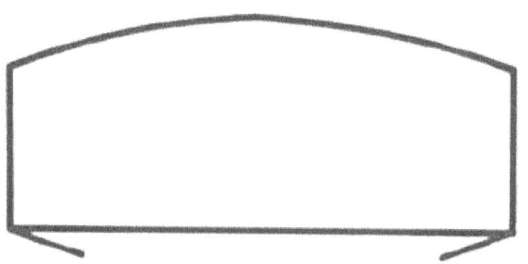
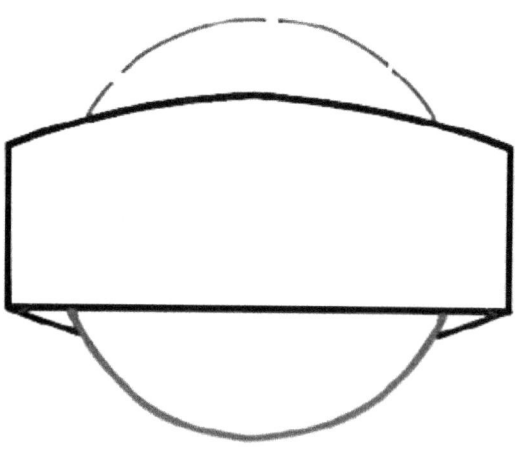

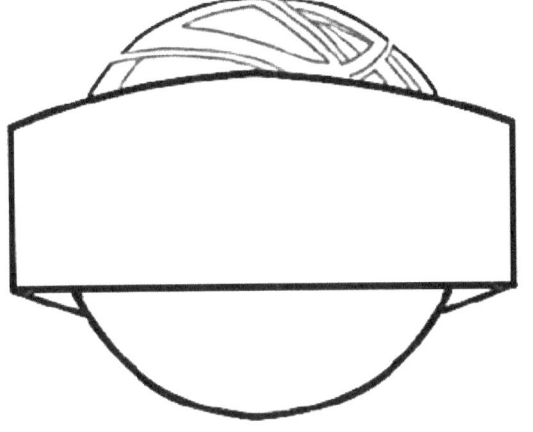

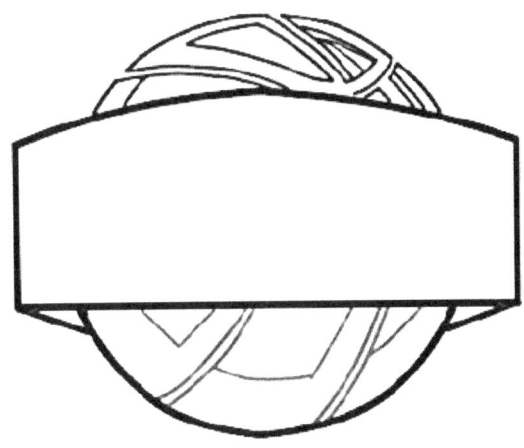

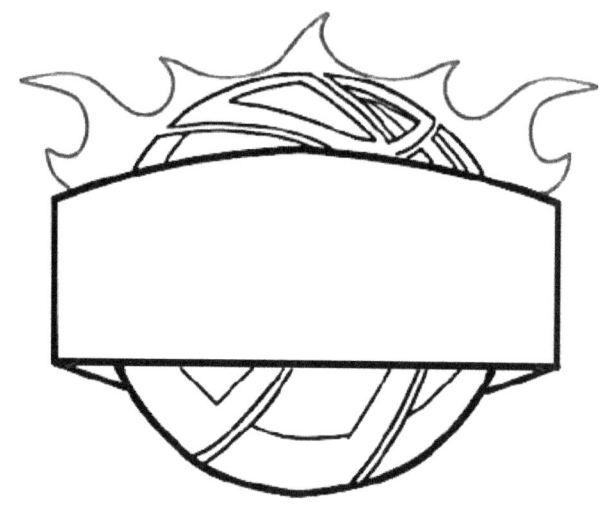
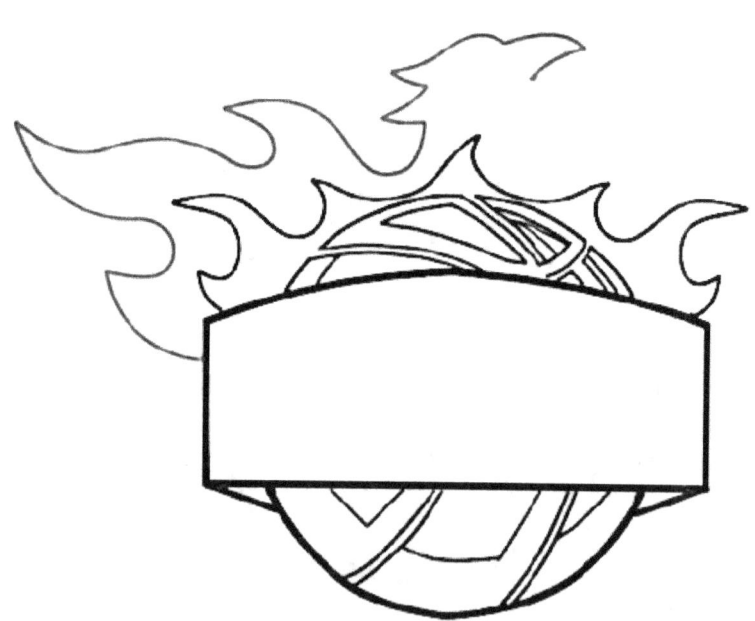

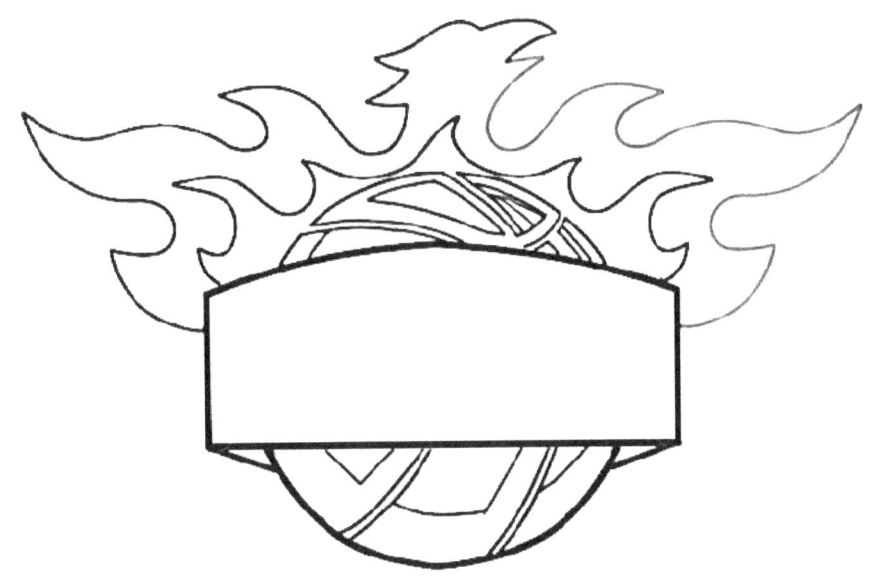
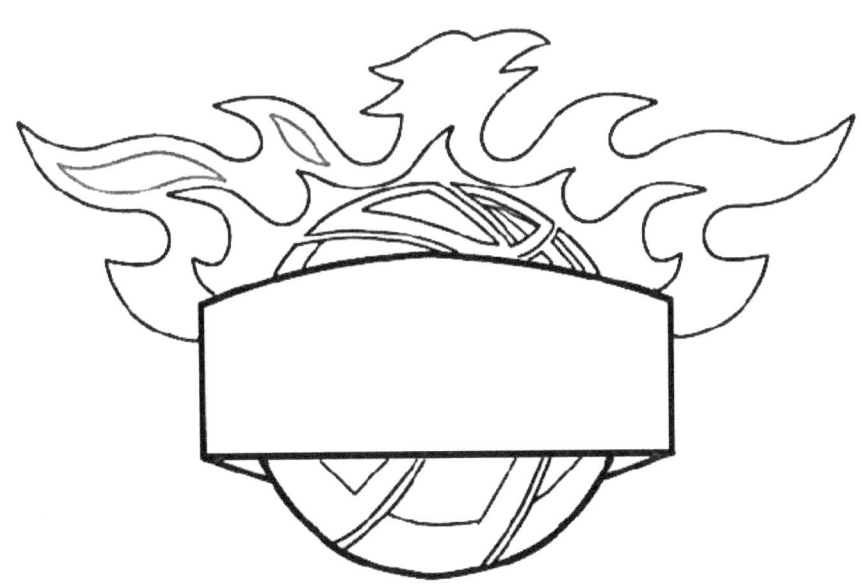

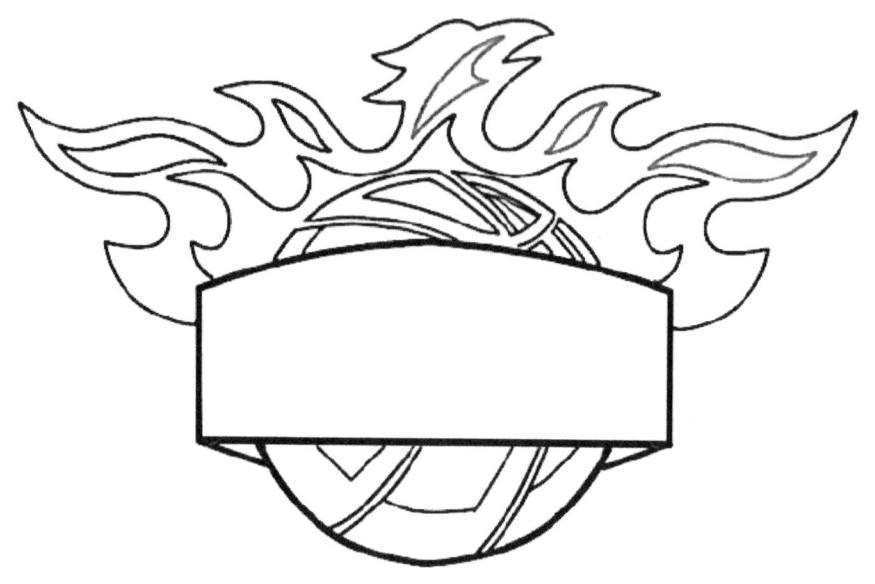
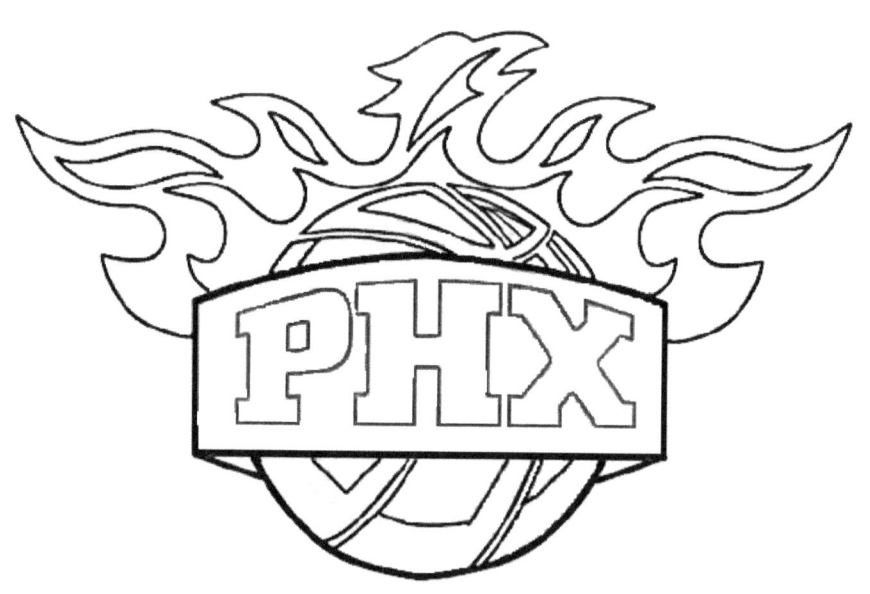

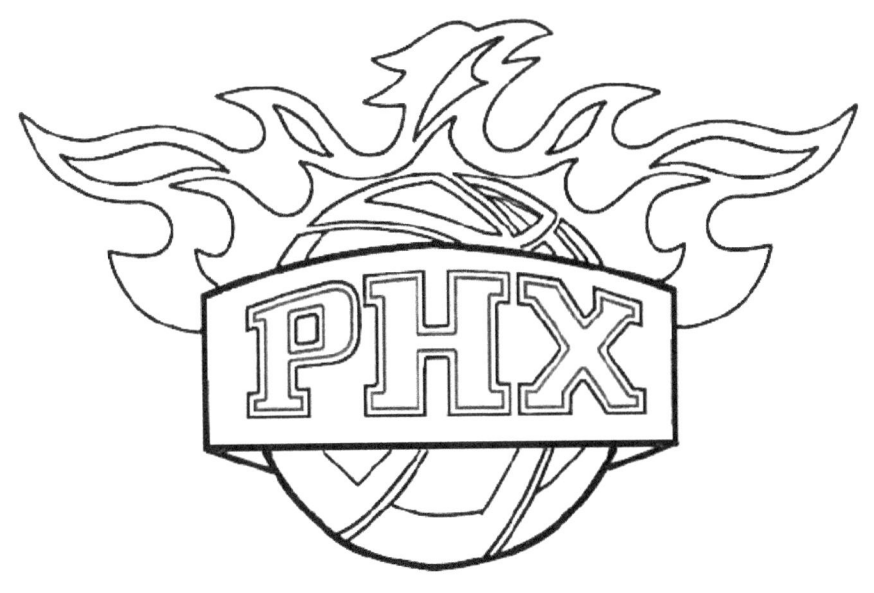

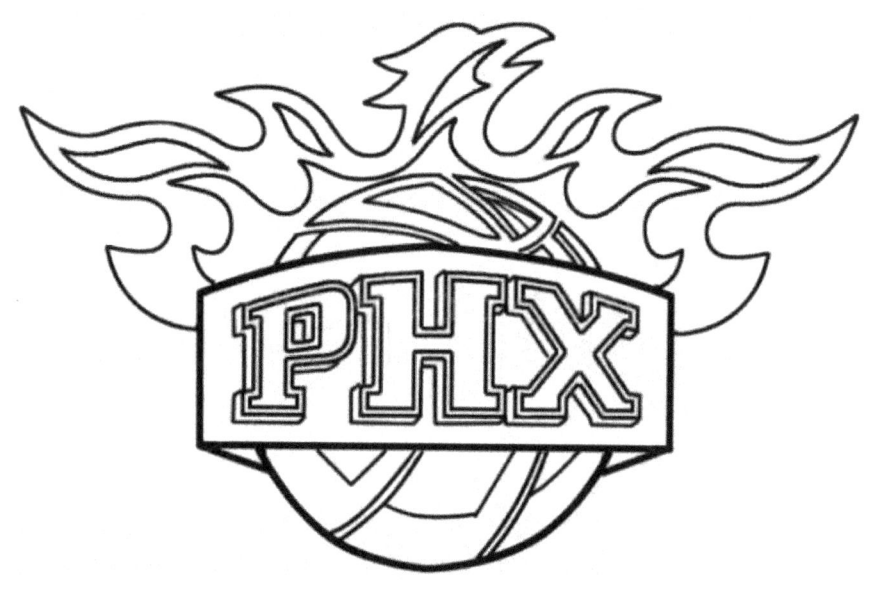

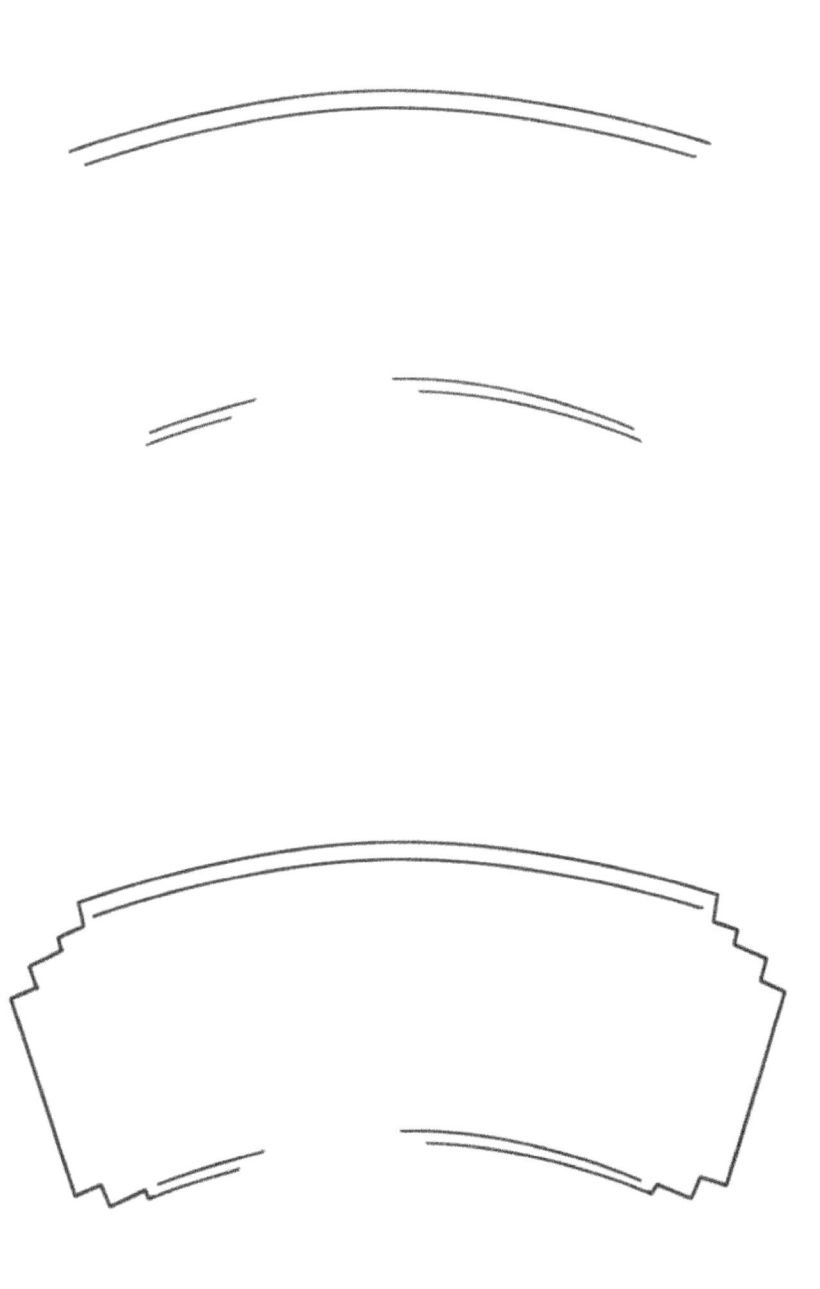

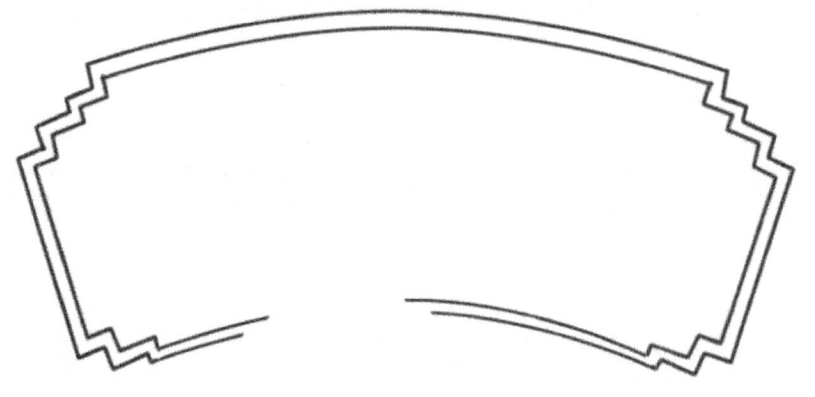
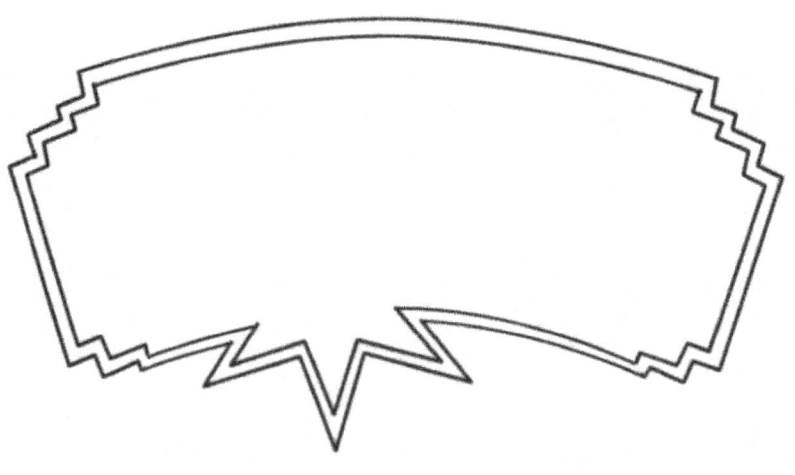

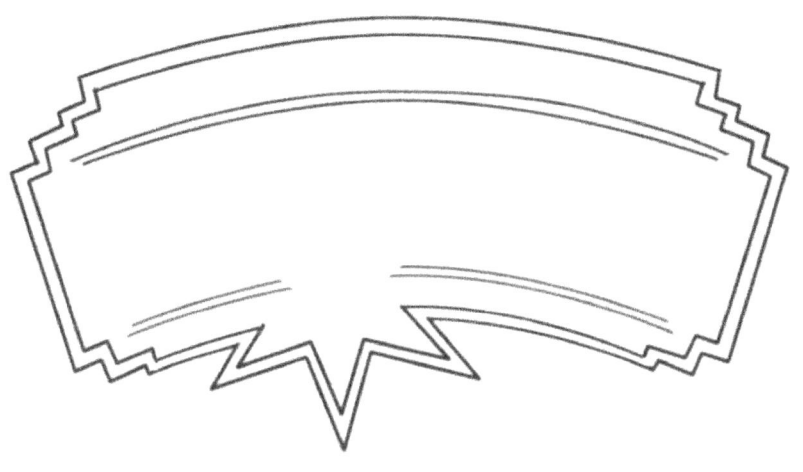
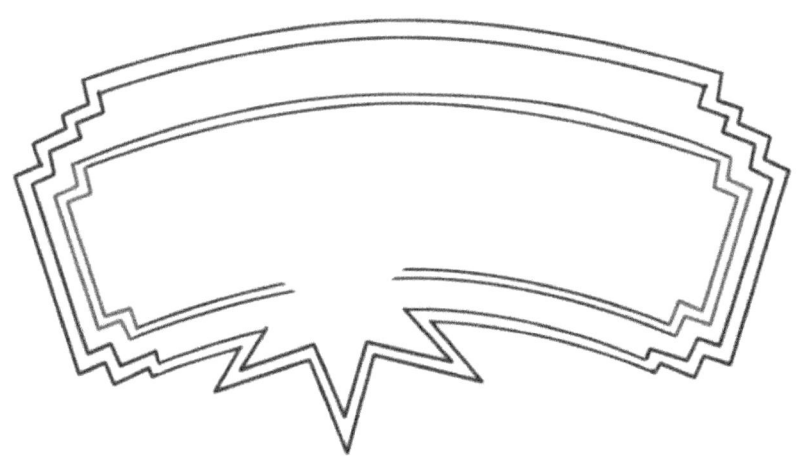

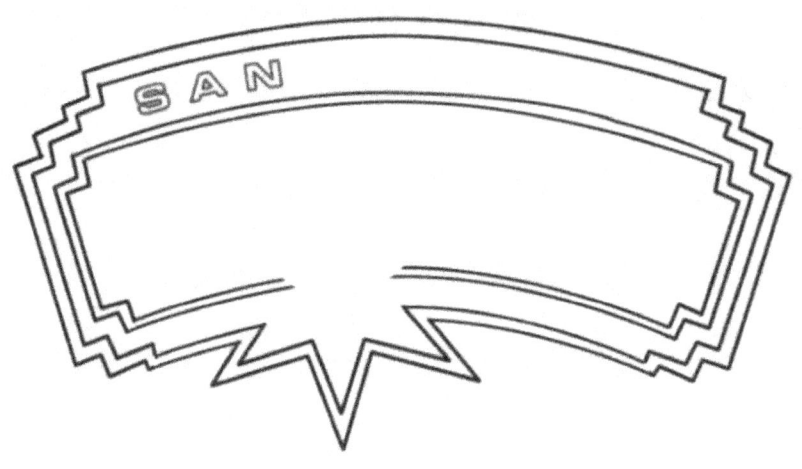
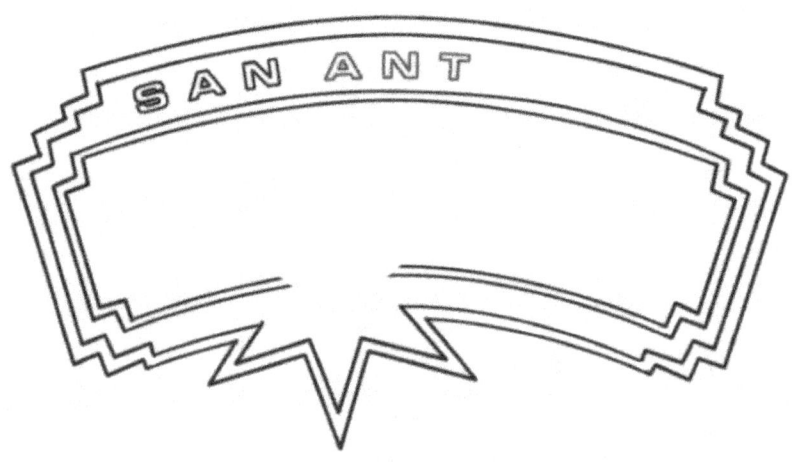

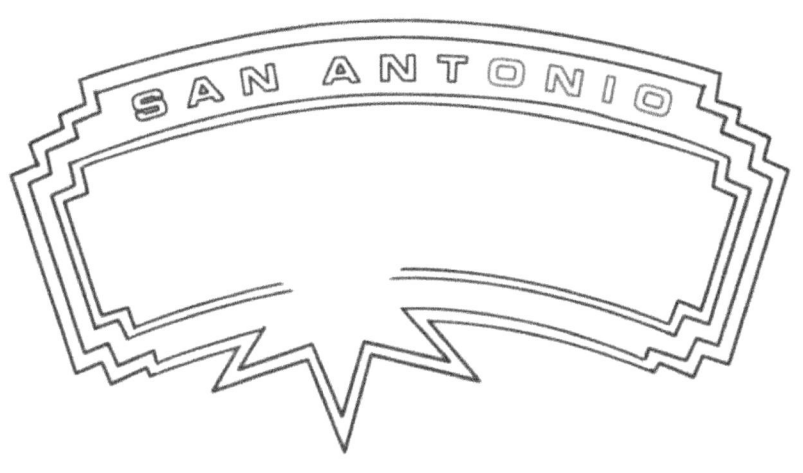

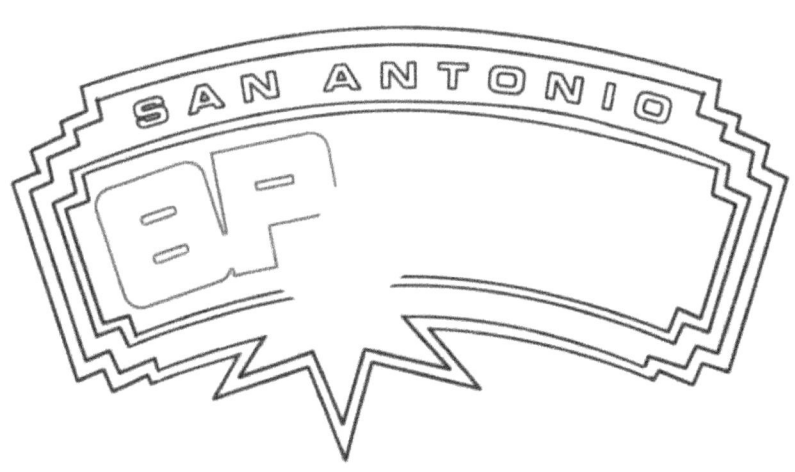

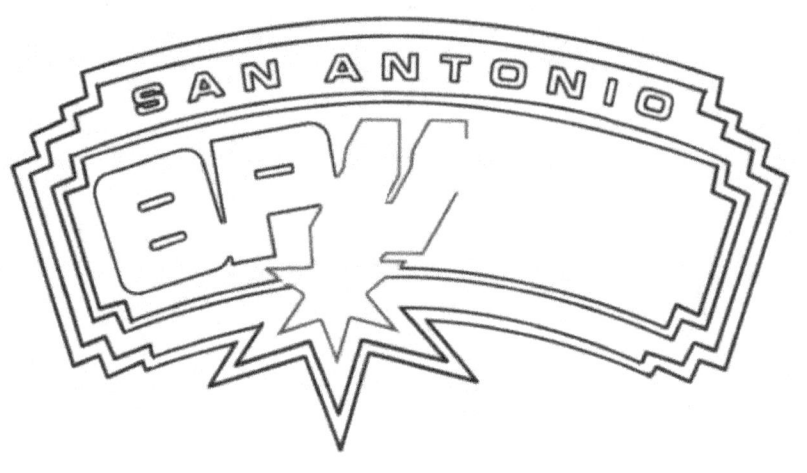

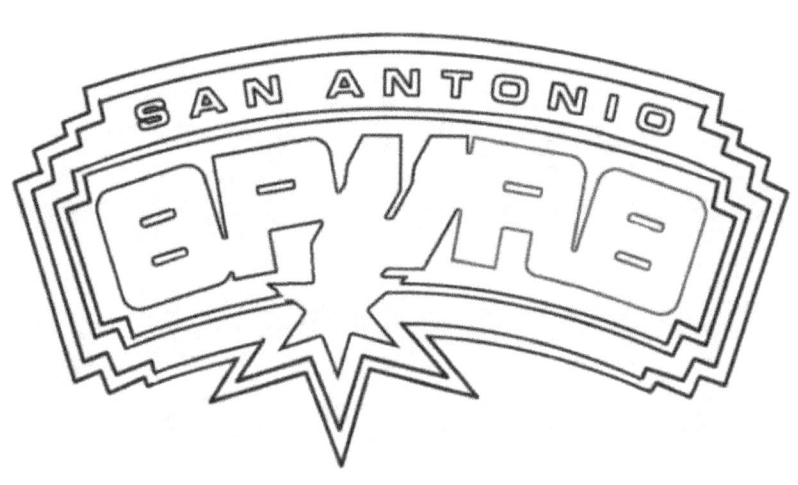

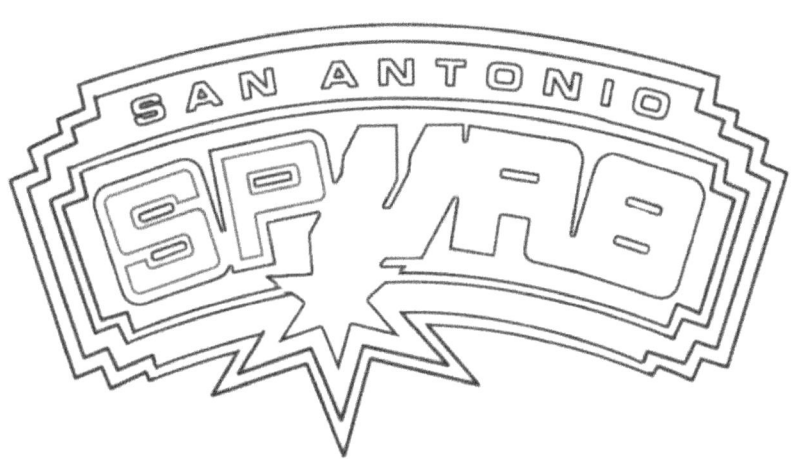

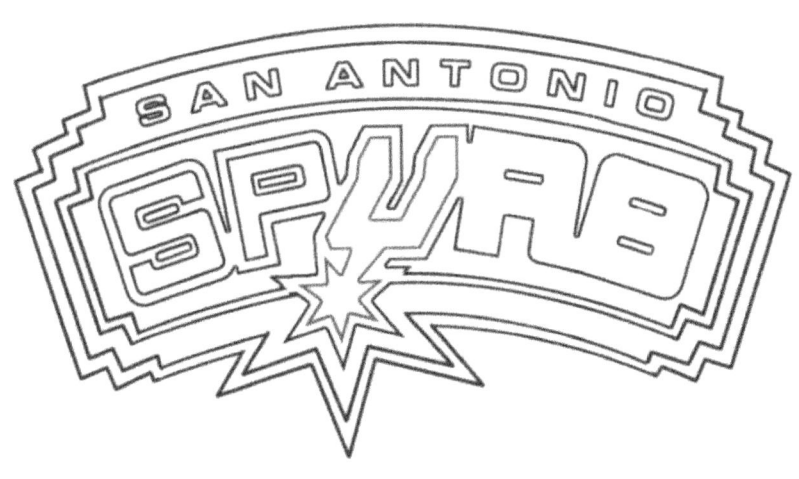

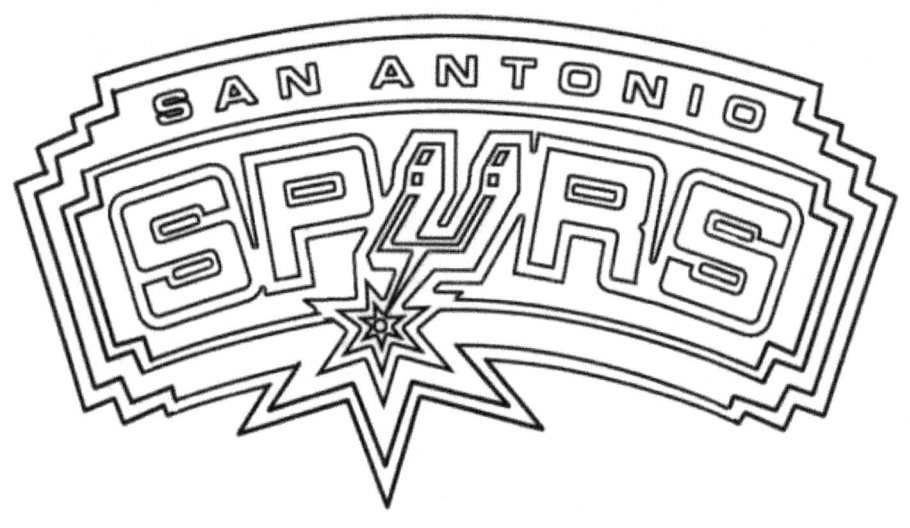

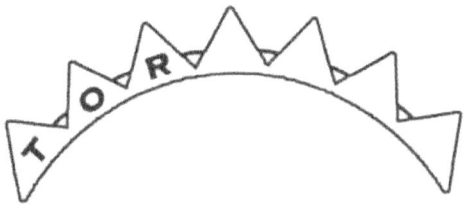

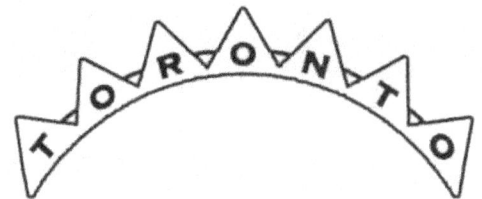

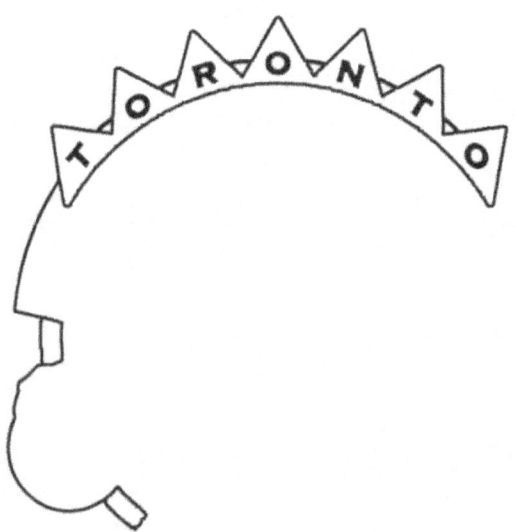

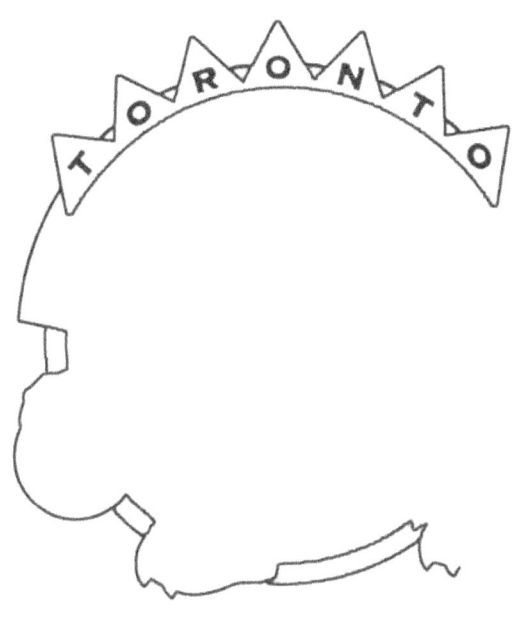
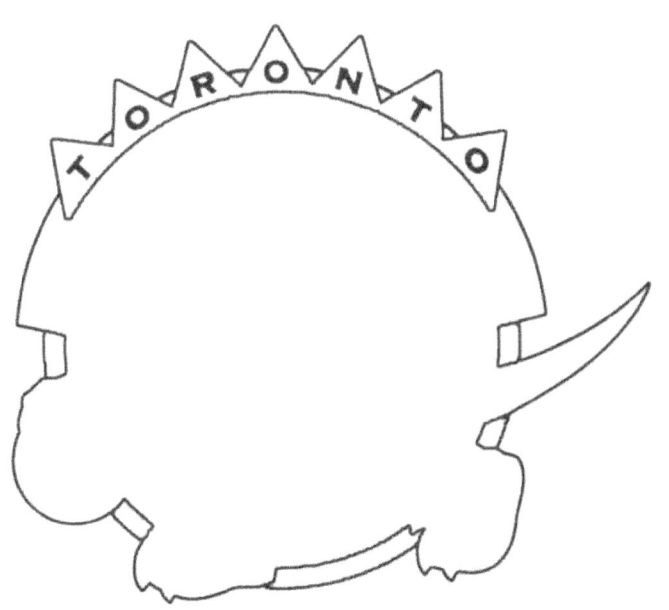

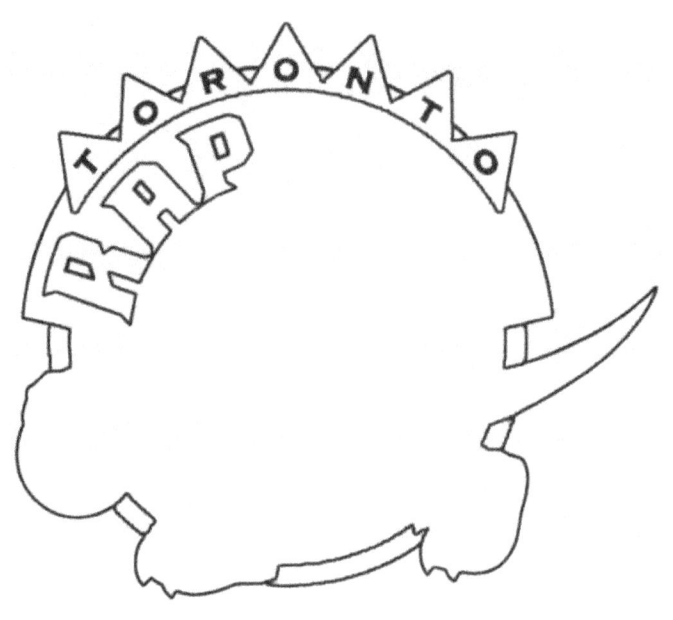

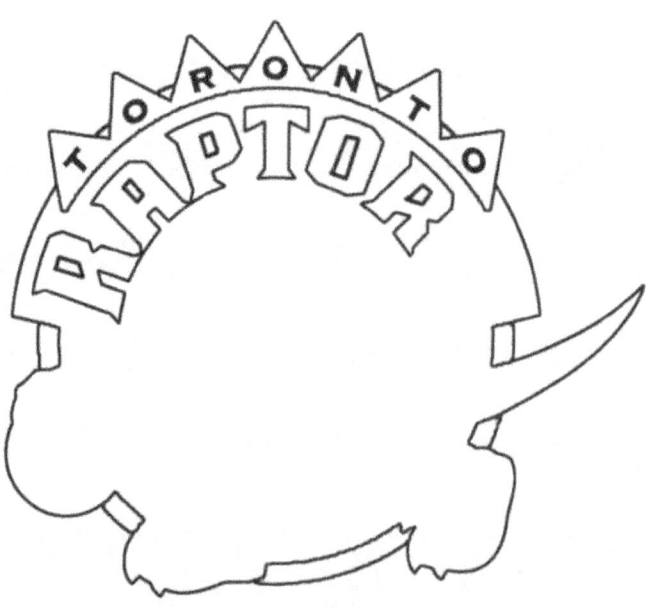

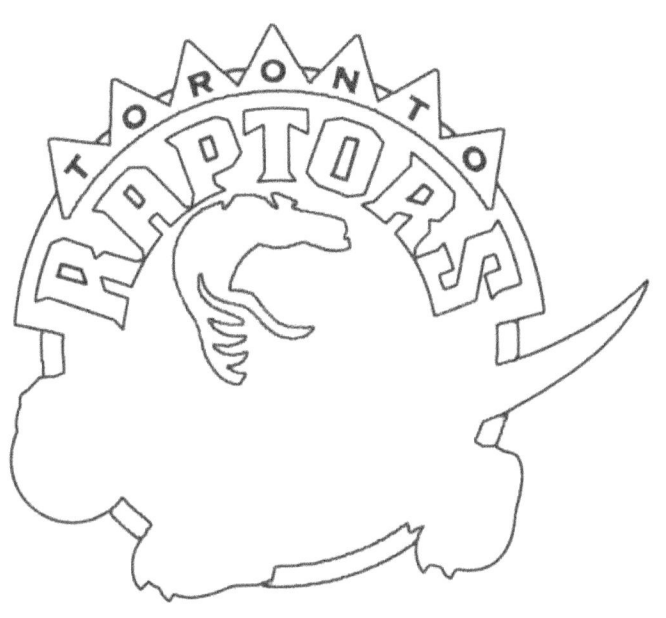

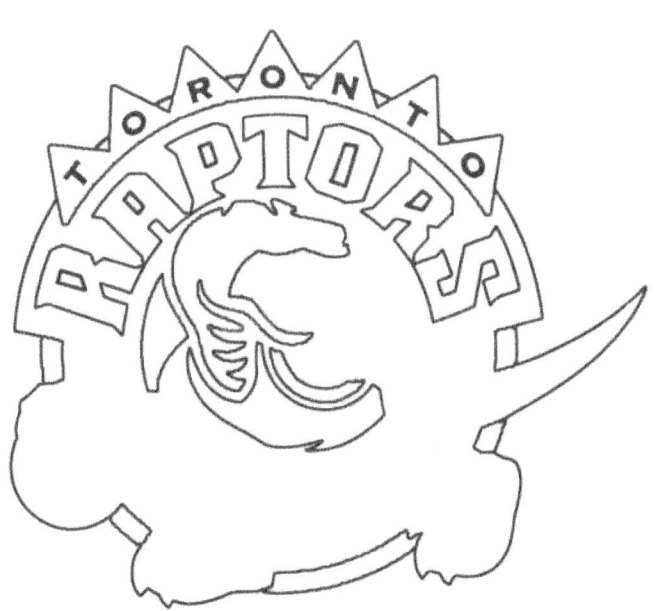

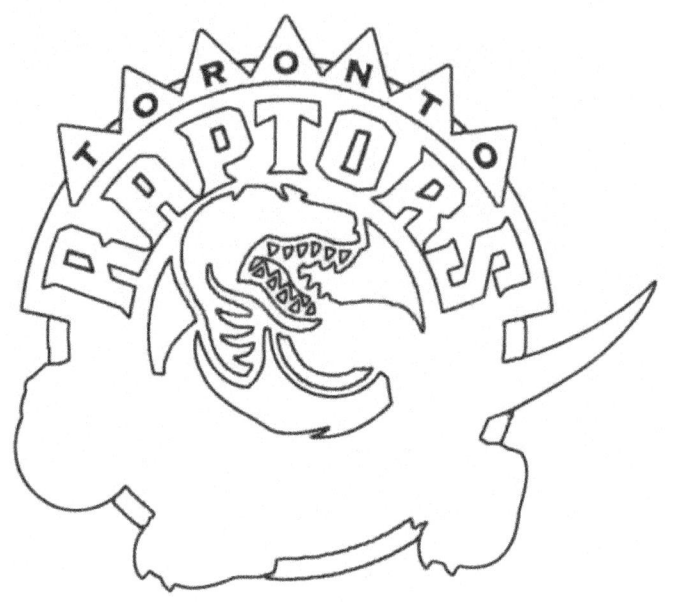
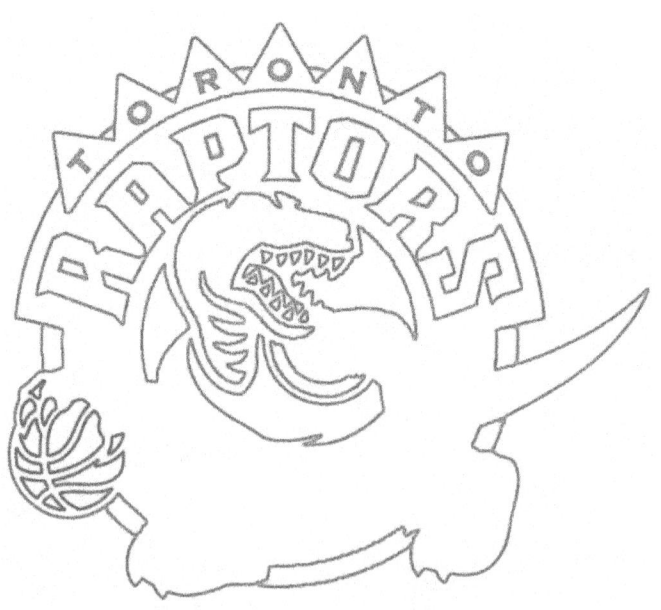

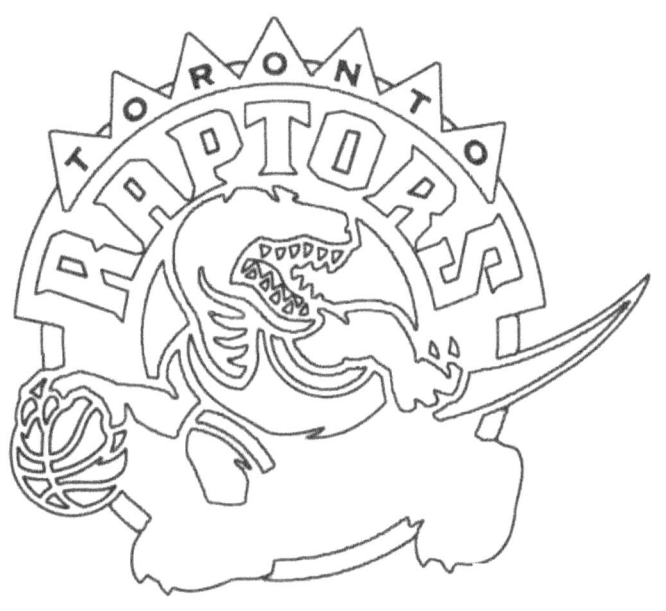

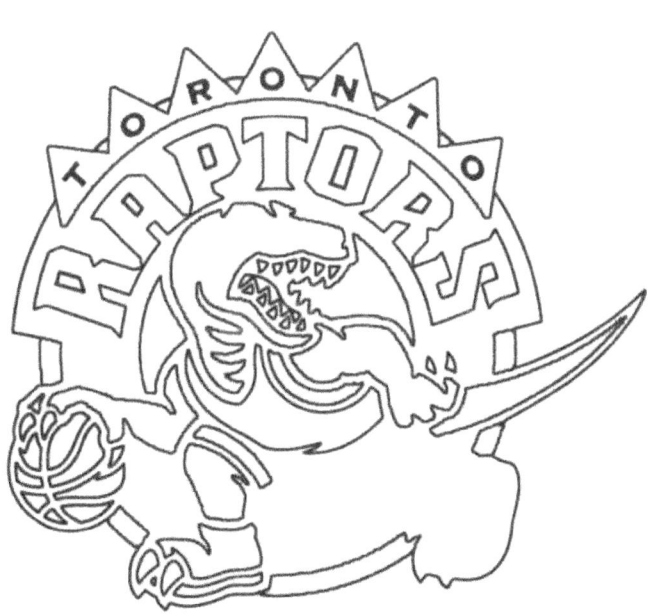

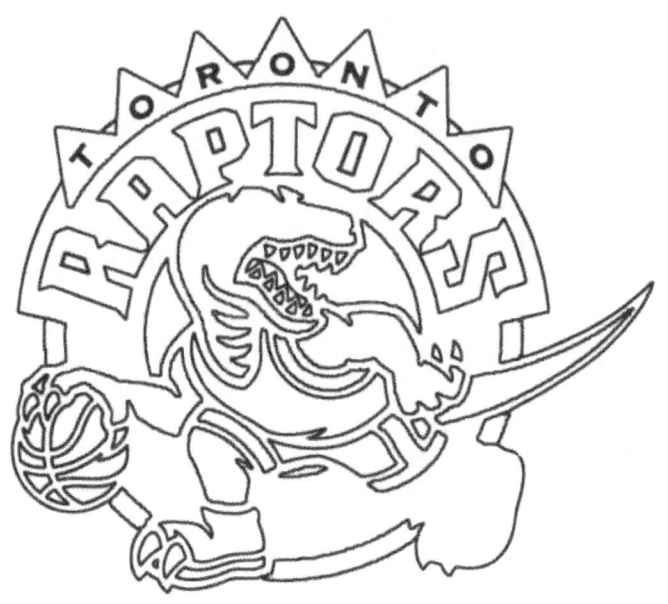
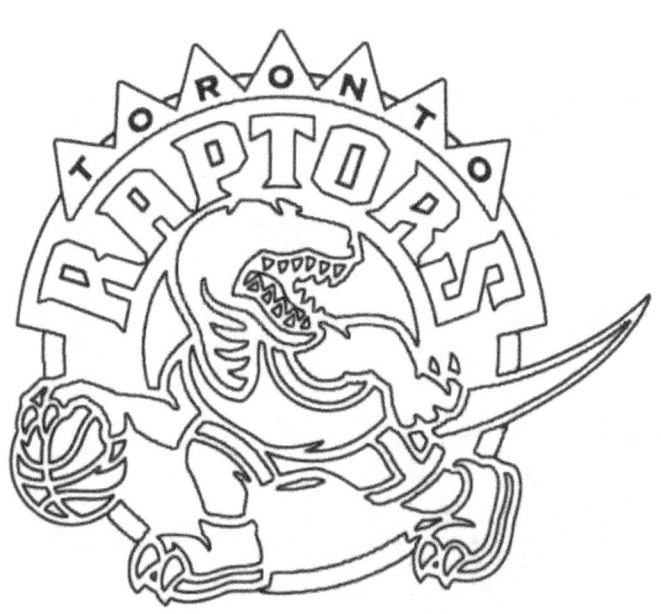

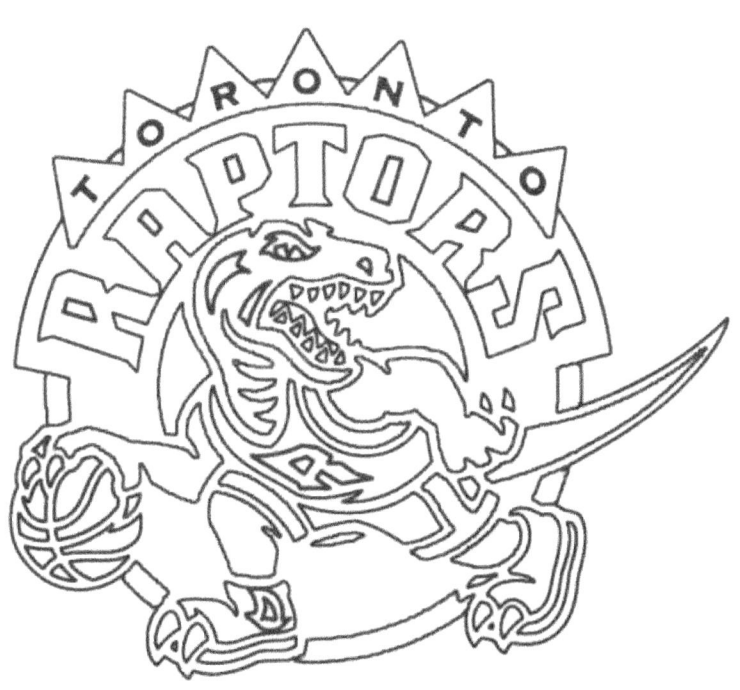

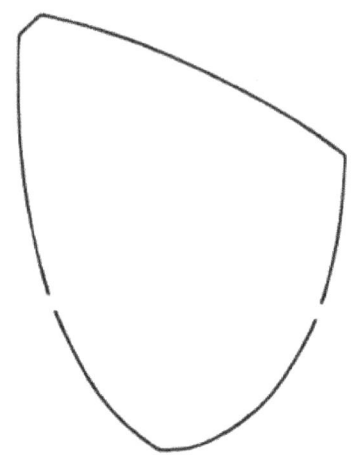

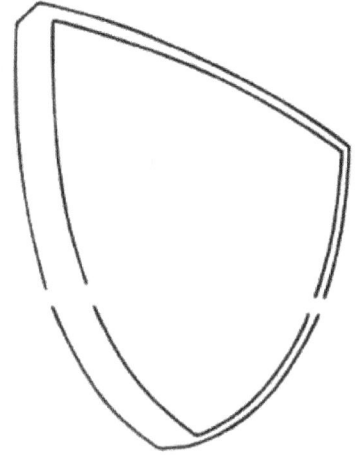

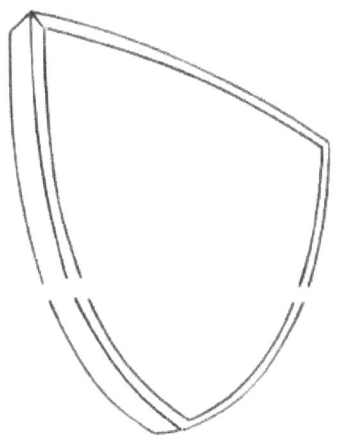

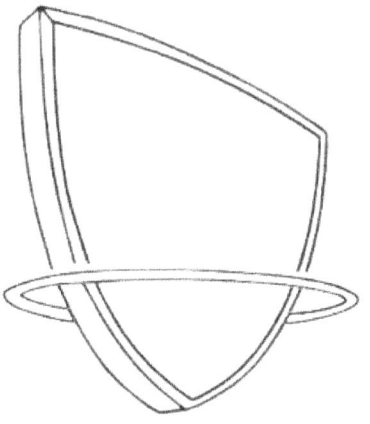

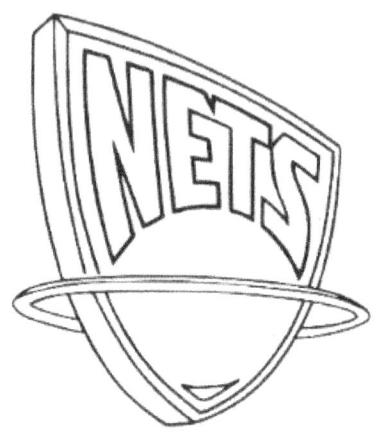

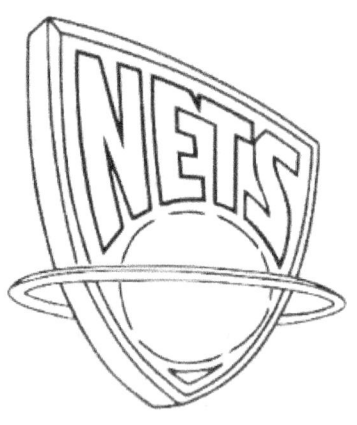

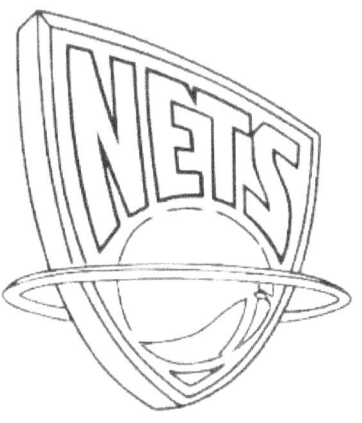
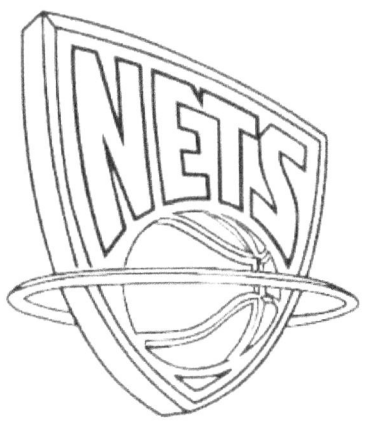

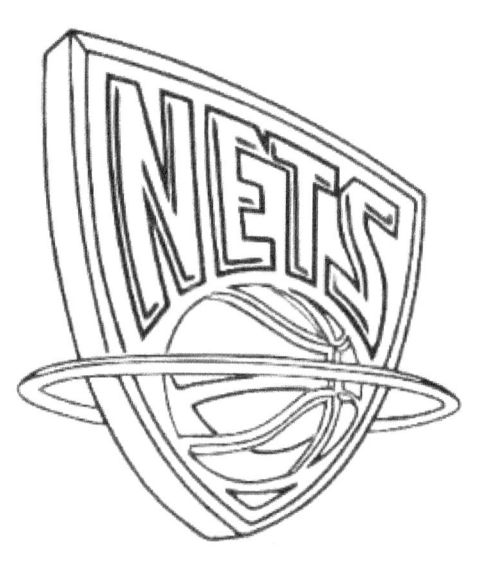

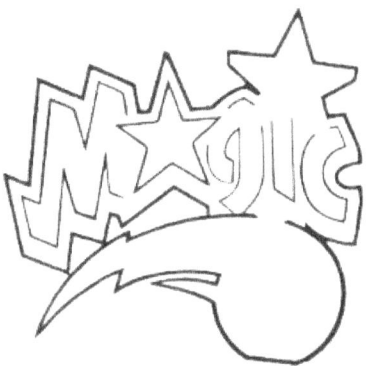

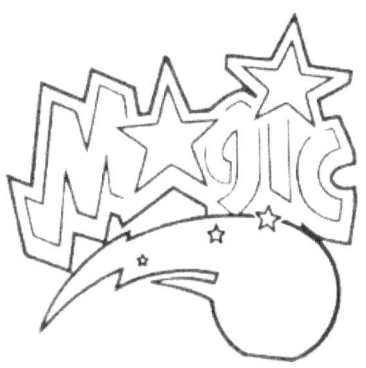

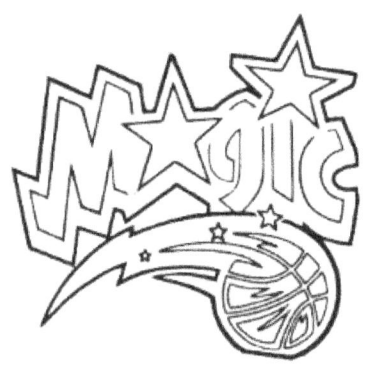

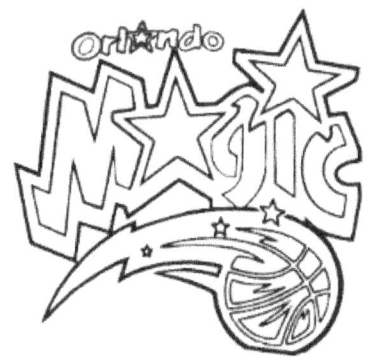

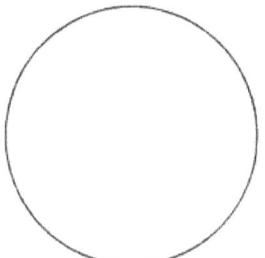

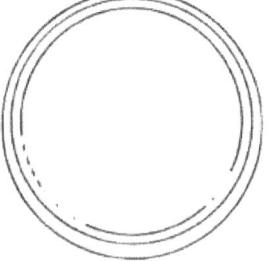

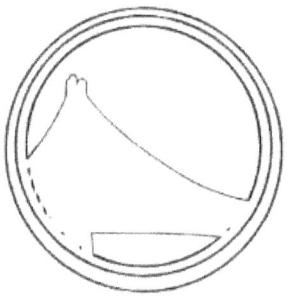

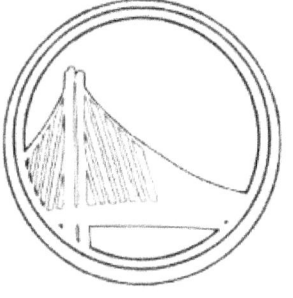

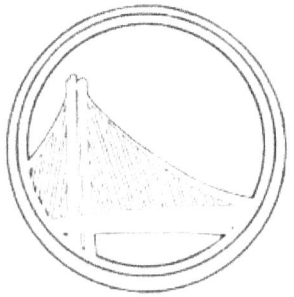

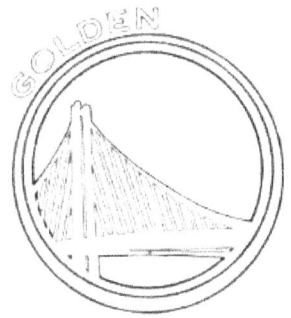

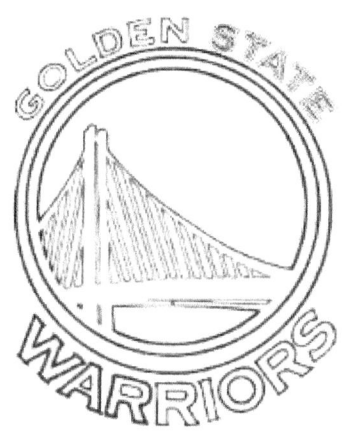

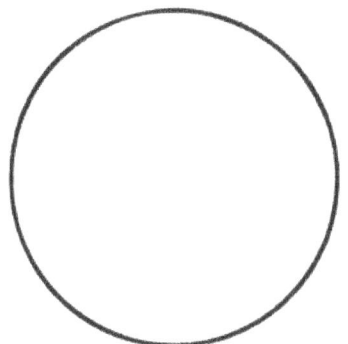

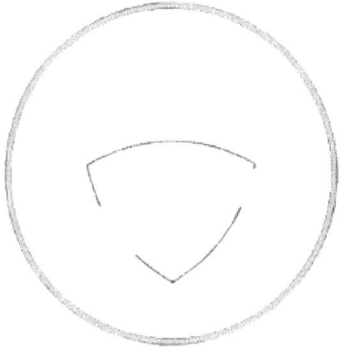

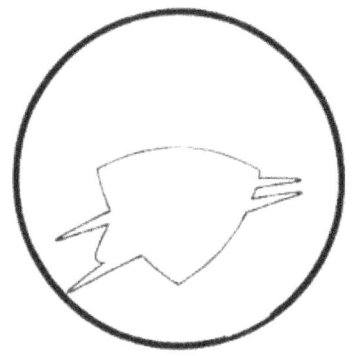

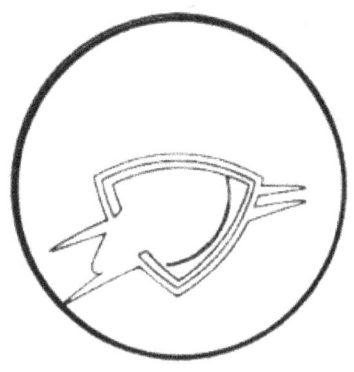

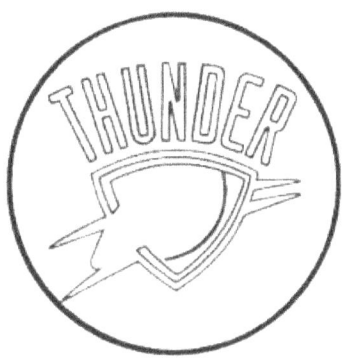

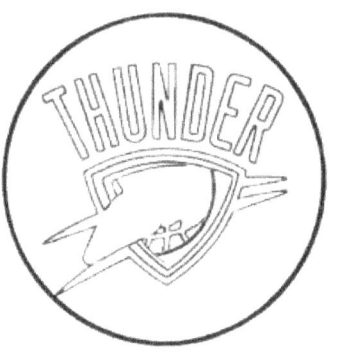

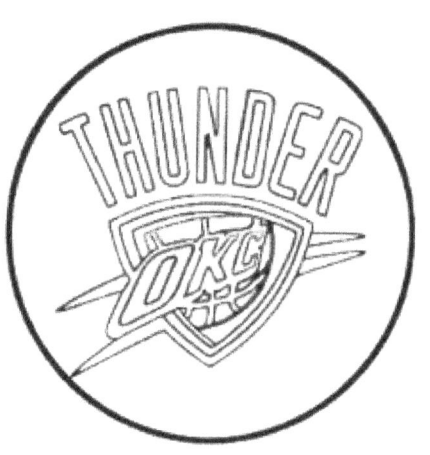

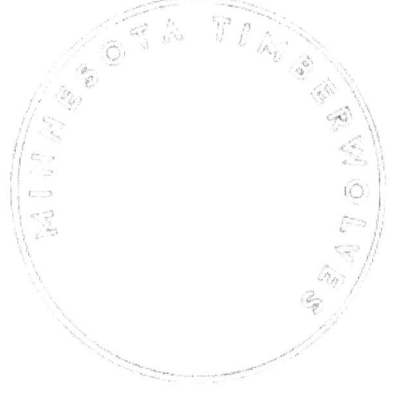

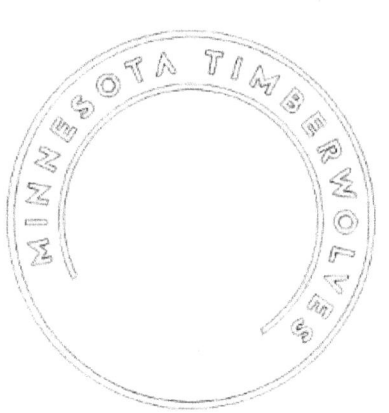

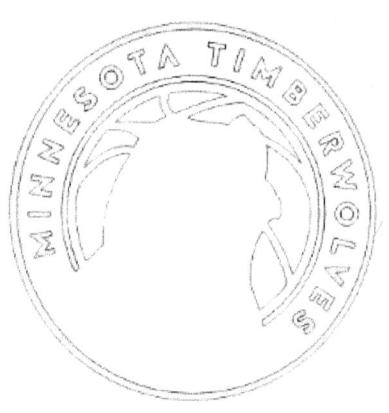

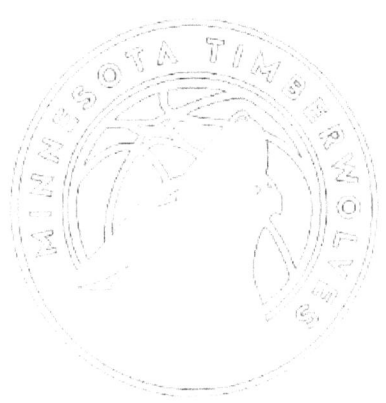
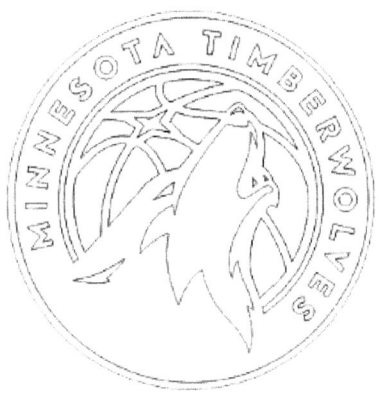

www.ingramcontent.com/pod-product-compliance
Lightning Source LLC
Chambersburg PA
CBHW070243220526
45465CB00004B/1511